Palgrave Studies in Economic History

Series Editor
Kent Deng, London School of Economics, London, UK

Palgrave Studies in Economic History is designed to illuminate and enrich our understanding of economies and economic phenomena of the past. The series covers a vast range of topics including financial history, labour history, development economics, commercialisation, urbanisation, industrialisation, modernisation, globalisation, and changes in world economic orders.

Sergi Basco · Jordi Domènech · Joan R. Rosés

Pandemics, Economics and Inequality

Lessons from the Spanish Flu

Sergi Basco
Department of Economics
University of Barcelona
Barcelona, Spain

Jordi Domènech
Department of Social Sciences
Universidad Carlos III de Madrid
Getafe (Madrid), Spain

Joan R. Rosés
Department of Economic History
London School of Economics
London, UK

ISSN 2662-6497   ISSN 2662-6500   (electronic)
Palgrave Studies in Economic History
ISBN 978-3-031-05667-3   ISBN 978-3-031-05668-0   (eBook)
https://doi.org/10.1007/978-3-031-05668-0

© The Author(s), under exclusive license to Springer Nature Switzerland AG 2022
This work is subject to copyright. All rights are solely and exclusively licensed by the Publisher, whether the whole or part of the material is concerned, specifically the rights of translation, reprinting, reuse of illustrations, recitation, broadcasting, reproduction on microfilms or in any other physical way, and transmission or information storage and retrieval, electronic adaptation, computer software, or by similar or dissimilar methodology now known or hereafter developed.
The use of general descriptive names, registered names, trademarks, service marks, etc. in this publication does not imply, even in the absence of a specific statement, that such names are exempt from the relevant protective laws and regulations and therefore free for general use.
The publisher, the authors, and the editors are safe to assume that the advice and information in this book are believed to be true and accurate at the date of publication. Neither the publisher nor the authors or the editors give a warranty, expressed or implied, with respect to the material contained herein or for any errors or omissions that may have been made. The publisher remains neutral with regard to jurisdictional claims in published maps and institutional affiliations.

Cover credit: Sean Gladwell

This Palgrave Macmillan imprint is published by the registered company Springer Nature Switzerland AG
The registered company address is: Gewerbestrasse 11, 6330 Cham, Switzerland

Per a la Claudia, l'Andrea, l'Àlex, el Maties, el Tomàs i la Sophie, que va néixer durant l'escriptura del llibre

Contents

1 **Introduction**   1
   Pandemics Throughout History   2
   Why a Book on the Spanish Flu?   7
   Plan of the Book   13
   References   15

2 **The Spanish Flu: A Global Shock**   17
   Origins and Chronology of the Pandemic   18
   Spanish Flu in the News   20
   Public Interventions   25
   A Global Shock with Local Effects   27
   References   30

3 **Unequal Mortality During the Spanish Flu**   33
   Computing Mortality During Pandemics   34
   Unequal Mortality During the Spanish Flu   36
   Social Distancing and Mortality   43
   References   46

4 **The Spanish Flu and the Labour Market**   51
   Pandemics and Wages: The Malthusian View   51
   The Spanish Flu and Real Wages   54
   References   62

5	The Spanish Flu and the Capital Market	65
	Pandemics and Capital Returns	65
	Pre-industrial Pandemics and Land Rents	66
	Modern Pandemics and Housing	69
	The 1918 Flu and Housing: Evidence from Spain	72
	References	80
6	Taking Stock: The Aggregate Effects of the Spanish Flu	83
	Aggregate Effects of Pandemics	83
	What Have We Learnt from Past Pandemics?	88
	Pandemics in the Pre-industrial World	88
	The Spanish Flu	90
	COVID vs Spanish Flu: A First Assessment	94
	References	100

References 105

Index 119

LIST OF FIGURES

Fig. 1.1	The GDP shock of the Spanish Flu versus the Great Recession	10
Fig. 2.1	Evolution of flu-related excess mortality in Spain	20
Fig. 2.2	Evolution of flu-related mentions in Spanish newspapers	22
Fig. 2.3	Evolution of "influenza" News in British newspapers	23
Fig. 3.1	Flu-related excess mortality by age and gender in Spain	38
Fig. 3.2	Determinants of flu-related excess mortality in Spain	40
Fig. 3.3	Flu-related excess mortality across occupations in Spain	41
Fig. 3.4	Flu-related excess mortality in urban and rural locations in Spain	43
Fig. 4.1	Theoretical effect of pandemics on real wages	57
Fig. 5.1	Theoretical effect of pandemics on the housing market	71
Fig. 5.2	Effect of the flu on mortgage markets in Spain	78
Fig. 6.1	Theoretical effect of pandemics on aggregate output	85
Fig. 6.2	Aggregate effect of the flu in Spain	86

List of Tables

Table 1.1	List of pandemics with the highest normalized death toll	3
Table 1.2	Global spread of the Spanish Flu	9
Table 4.1	Effect of the Spanish Flu on real wages in Spain, by occupation	59
Table 5.1	Effects of the flu on urban house prices in Spain	75
Table 6.1	Effects of the flu on output in Spain	93

CHAPTER 1

Introduction

Abstract Why a book on the Spanish Flu? Pandemics are deadly diseases that happen simultaneously in several countries and affect a substantial fraction of the population. The Spanish Flu, with a global death toll ranging from 50 to 100 million, was one of the deadliest pandemics in history. Moreover, the substantial economic crisis generated by the Spanish Flu also deserves careful examination. Lastly, the outburst of the Covid-19 has increased the interest in the Spanish Flu, which is the closest pandemic in terms of timing, spread, and global death toll. This book provides a comprehensive and unified overview of the economic effects of the 1918 influenza, with special emphasis on the Spanish economy, from which we hand-collected new data. It also explains why its consequences may be different from other pandemics like the ongoing Covid-19 pandemic and the Black Death.

Keywords Spanish Flu · Great Recession · Pandemics · Economic crises · Death toll

Pandemics Throughout History

The Merriam-Webster dictionary defines a pandemic as "an outbreak of a disease that occurs over a wide geographic area (such as multiple countries or continents) and typically affects a significant proportion of the population".[1] Therefore, candidate events need to meet two requirements to be qualified as pandemics: (1) they need to be global and (2) they need to affect a substantial amount of people.

Table 1.1 provides a ranking of pandemics according to their global mortality impact. One hurdle when comparing pandemics across time is that the world population has increased considerably over time. It means that, for example, one death in year 165 (the start of Antonine Plague) should count relatively more than one death of Covid-19 in the year 2020. In other words, to compare across pandemics, we need to normalize the total number of deaths during each episode by the world population at the time. A second problem constructing this ranking is that, even though there has been substantial progress in measuring population over time due to the efforts of several generations of cliometricians, data about older episodes are still best guesses. It is not only about the reliability of the mortality data but, even more importantly, about how to impute these deaths to the pandemic. In Chapter 3, we discuss in detail these methodological issues applied to the Spanish Flu. However, these measurement problems are even more significant for the older plagues. For this chapter, we take the normalized death tolls reported in Cirillo and Taleb (2020). We refer the reader to this paper for more details.

The most ancient epidemic reported in Cirillo and Taleb (2020) is the Plague of Athens, which took place between 429 and 426 BC. The most recent pandemic, which is still ongoing at the time of the writing of this book, is Covid-19.

The first pandemic in Table 1.1 is the deadliest and most famous one: The Black Death (1331–1353). This pandemic claimed between 75 and 200 million lives. According to the normalized average estimate reported in Cirillo and Taleb (2020), it would represent a death toll of 2.678 million today. In other words, it would kill around one-third of the overall world population. We know that it was a bubonic plague.[2] An infectious disease caused by the Yersinia Pestis; a bacterium transmitted from rodents to humans. The most common transmission channel was the bite of an infected flea.[3]

Table 1.1 List of pandemics with the highest normalized death toll

Name	Year	Location	Disease	Death toll (average estimate)	Death toll normalized
Black Death	1331–1353	Eurasia, North Africa	Plague	137,500	2,678,283
Plague of Justinian	541–542	Mediterranean, Europe, Near East	Plague	62,500	2,246,550
Antonine Plague	165–180	Roman Empire	Unknown	7,500	283,355
Spanish Flu	**1918–1920**	**Worldwide**	**Influenza**	**58,500**	**193,789**
Cocoliztli Epidemic	1545–1548	Mexico	Unknown	10,000	165,668
Third Plague Pandemic	1855–1960	Worldwide	Plague	18,500	111,986
Smallpox Epidemic	1520–1520	Mexico	Smallpox	6,500	107,684
Smallpox Epidemic	735–737	Japan	Smallpox	2,000	67,690
HIV/AIDS Pandemic	1981–2020	Worldwide	HIV/AIDS	30,000	61,768
Covid-19	2019–2021[a]	Worldwide	Sars-CoV-2	16,200[b]	16,200[b]

Notes Death toll numbers are in thousands. Death toll normalized is the rescaled measure of the average estimates in Cirillo and Taleb (2020) using coeval population (see cited article for details). (a) Pandemic was still ongoing at the time of the writing of the book. (b) The Economist estimates that the global excess mortality of Covid-19 is 16.2 million. https://www.economist.com/leaders/2021/10/16/millions-of-lives-depend-on-how-the-pandemic-ends

Christakos et al. (2005) provide a detailed account of the diffusion and mortality of the Black Death. The data seem to indicate that the city of Messina in Sicily was the entry point of the plague in Europe. From there, the plague spread rapidly following trade routes. Mortality was higher during the early stages of the outbreak, before the population gained immunity or the disease mutated. Jedwab et al. (2021) show that some regions were hit harder by the plague than others. The Black Death caused the highest mortality in Italy, France, Portugal, Spain, England, and the Scandinavian countries. Instead, Central and Eastern Europe experienced relatively low mortality rates. Contrary to the popular belief, cities were not more affected than the countryside.

Why was mortality so high during the Black Death? Jedwab et al. (2021) summarize the different explanations. First, overpopulation in Western Europe made the population vulnerable and facilitated the spread of the Black Death. Second, Europeans did not have immune protection against this Plague, due to their historical isolation from the focus of the Yersinia Pestis in Central Asia. Third, the omnipresence of black rats facilitated the rapid diffusion of the illness. Finally, society could not develop adequate public health of medical answers to the Plague. Since the Black Death is the pandemic with the highest death toll, most of the consensus on the economic effects of pandemics derive from the analysis of this event. We will review the evidence on the effects of the Black Death in several chapters of this book.

The second most deadly pandemic was the Plague of Justinian (541–542). As can be seen in Table 1.1, the normalized death toll was 2.246 million people. Note that even though it is not as popular as the Black Death, it seems to have had a comparable effect in terms of global mortality. As the name suggests, the plague was its cause. Justinian I, the Byzantine emperor from 527 to 565, gives his name to this plague. The pandemic spread outside the Byzantine Empire towards Europe, the Near East, and the Mediterranean countries. Popular accounts have related the Plague of Justinian with the fall of Rome because the arrival of the plague coincided with the presence of the Justinian army in Italy.[4] New research has not only softened the link between the Justinian Plague and its long-run effects on the transformation of Europe, but it has also cast doubts on the "exaggerated" mortality numbers of this plague.[5]

The next pandemic on the list is the Antonine Plague (165–168). The normalized death toll was significantly lower than the first two, around 283 million (Table 1.1). The label of the pandemic is due to emperor

Antoninus Pius. Even though this event is known as Antonine Plague, it does not seem to be caused by the plague. Indeed, the cause could have been virologic rather than bacterial, being measles and smallpox the two major candidates. Literature has also agreed that the substantial mortality was due to a lack of previous exposure to the disease. The coverage of the pandemic was the Roman empire. There exist contrasting views on the effects of the plague on the fate of the Roman Empire. As emphasized in Gilliam (1961), whereas some earlier notable scholars, like Barthold George Niebuhr (1776–1831), thought of the plague as a turning point for the Roman Empire; more recent scholars, including himself, are more sceptical on how decisive this event was for Rome.

Next in the ranking is the Spanish Flu (1918–1920),[6] the main topic of this book. It was a worldwide pandemic caused by influenza. As it is well known, influenza is a virus. It is transmitted commonly between persons by air when infected people cough, sneeze, or talk. The prevalent variant of influenza during the Spanish Flu was A/H1N1. The name of the Spanish Flu is a misnomer: the pandemic did not emerge in Spain, but the Spanish press was the first to inform about its existence.[7] As discussed above, its death toll remains today uncertain. The average estimate used in Cirillo and Taleb (2020) is 58.5 million deaths, which is equivalent to 283 million people today. However, if we take the upper estimate of 100 million (the same as in Johnson & Mueller, 2002), the normalized number of deaths would be above 330 million. In this case, the Spanish Flu would climb to the top-3 of the deadliest pandemics in history.

In the fifth position, there is the Cocolitztli Epidemic (1545–1548).[8] This pandemic took place in Mexico and claimed the equivalent to 165 million people today. There exists no consensus on the actual disease behind this pandemic, albeit smallpox is the most likely suspect. New DNA-based research shows that, at least, salmonella was one of the pathogens present in sixteenth-century Mexico.[9] The Mexican smallpox pandemic (1519–1520), number seven in Table 1.1, could be part of the same event.[10] This pandemic and the 1519–1520 smallpox epidemic have been linked to the arrival of the Spanish invaders to Mexico.[11] Then, it is plausible that Spaniards brought with them some bacteria and viruses that killed the previously unexposed native population. Acuña-Soto et al. (2002) also argue that extreme drought conditions exacerbated the mortality of the Cocoliztli. However, there are some accounts that Spaniards, and black slaves, were not immune since some died from the mysterious disease (Prem, 1991).

The Third Plague Pandemic (1855–1960) ranks sixth in Table 1.1. It is called the third plague pandemic after the Plague of Justinian and the Black Death, which we discussed above. As in these other pandemics, it was due to the plague. One particularity of this plague is the extended time horizon and the several outbreaks in different countries. It was originated in the Yunnan region of China with several episodes since 1772. However, it was not until it reached Hong Kong that it quickly spread across the globe. According to the data in Bramanti et al. (2019), the first European documented case was on the island of Chios (Greece) in 1893, and we also observe early accounts of the plague outbreaks in different European cities like Lisbon (1899), London (1900), Barcelona (1902), Marseille (1902), or Naples (1901). In London, there were plague outbreaks in 1900, 1905, 1910, 1917, 1918, 1919, and 1920. The last documented plague outbreak in Europe was in Taranto (Italy) in 1945. The normalized total death toll of the Third Plague Pandemic is around 112 million people. The death toll was below the Spanish Flu , and it was more dispersed over time. However, this number is uncertain because the literature has ignored this pandemic, and it had multiple outbreaks in different countries and times.

The smallpox epidemic of Japan (735–737) ranks eighth in Table 1.1. In normalized terms, 68 million people are the estimated death toll. During the following centuries, Japan continued to experience smallpox epidemics until this illness became endemic (Bowman, 2014). This pandemic killed between 25 and 35% of the Japanese population involving the whole society, including the nobility (Farris, 2020). This author also argues that this population debacle, and the subsequent smallpox outbursts, had substantial long-run effects in Japan since it resulted in an excess supply of land per inhabitant, which delayed technological innovation. In sum, his thesis is that smallpox pandemics held back ancient Japan and caused "economic backwardness". Even though the literature agrees on the population debacle during 737–737, some authors are more sceptical on the negative economic role of smallpox.[12] It seems that more research would be necessary to reach a definitive conclusion.

The ninth pandemic on the list is the HIV/AIDS Pandemic (1981–2020). The first reported case was in 1981, but the pandemic is still ongoing. For example, the World Health Organization (WHO) informs that, in 2020, 37.7 million people were living with HIV, and 680,000 people died of HIV-related causes.[13] The number reported in Table 1.1 (with data up to 2020) states that the normalized number of people that have died of HIV/AIDS is 61.7 million. Even though there are still HIV-related deaths across the globe, Africa concentrates a substantial part of mortality. According to WHO, in 2020, almost 70% of HIV-related deaths were in that continent. In contrast, deaths in Europe represented only 6% of the total. The geographic distribution of new HIV-infected is similar. Africa concentrates 60% of total cases, whereas Europe only the 11%.[14]

Given the prevalence of this pandemic in Africa, there have been several academic papers linking HIV/AIDS with the economic performance of the continent. Young (2005) argues that AIDS could increase welfare in Africa. He points out that HIV/AIDS has two main effects on the African economy: (1) decreases the human capital (education) of orphaned children, which reduces output, and (2) reduces the fertility rate, which reduces population and labour force. The fertility effect dominates and leads to higher income and consumption per capita, which become permanent. Kalemi-Ozcan and Turan (2011) challenge this result. These authors argue that, by using more recent surveys, the effect of HIV/AIDS prevalence on fertility is positive and, thus, this pandemic would decrease income per capita. Fortson (2011) provides further evidence on the negative effect of this pandemic in Africa. She documents that those countries with higher HIV/AIDS prevalence experience substantial declines in years of schooling, attendance, and completion of primary school. However, income per capita may not be a sufficient statistic of welfare. Jones and Klenow (2016) propose a new welfare measure that includes consumption, leisure, mortality, and inequality. If we employ this comprehensive welfare measure, Sub-Saharan Africa diverged even more from the rich countries. Arguably, the spread of HIV/AIDS contributes to this profound welfare divergence.

Why a Book on the Spanish Flu?

As we have seen, some pandemics have generated dramatic events such as institutional revolutions and technological change, which have led to dramatic changes in the income distribution. However, not all pandemics have the same economic and social effects. In this sense, this book has two main objectives: (1) to understand the economic consequences of pandemics and (2) to establish how the Spanish Flu fits into the general view on the benign long-run economic consequences of pandemics.

Importantly, we will emphasize that the Spanish Flu seems a more important reference point than the much-studied Black Death to forecast the economic consequences of Covid-19.

Table 1.2 shows that the Spanish Flu meets the requirements for being considered a pandemic. On the one hand, the Spanish Flu was a global event spreading all continents. In this table, we report data for selected countries in America, Africa, Asia, and Europe. On the other hand, we know that a considerable fraction of the world population was affected and died due to 1918 influenza. The global death toll ranged between 50 and 100 million people (Johnson & Mueller, 2002). These numbers imply that for every 1000 people in 1918, the Spanish Flu claimed between 2.5 and 5 lives. That mortality rate would have caused 200 million deaths in today's world population. For comparison with Covid-19, *The Economist* estimates that its global death toll is around 16.2 million people.[15] Therefore, the death toll of the Spanish Flu is one order of magnitude larger than the Covid-19 one.

Before going ahead with an in-depth analysis of the economic consequences of the 1918 influenza, it would be illuminating to compare it with another major economic shock. In this case, we have decided to compare the Spanish Flu with the Great Recession of 2008, the most recent global economic shock. To do so, Fig. 1.1 examines the evolution of real Gross Domestic Product (GDP) per capita before, during, and after the Spanish Flu (blue line) and the Great Recession (orange line) for some selected countries. To have comparable data across time and countries, we use data from the Madison Project.[16] The point O of the vertical line corresponds to the year 2008 for the Great Recession and 1918 for the Spanish Flu, respectively. We have selected these six countries because, as we will explain in later chapters, there is substantial research on the impact of the Spanish Flu on them.

Italy. Real GDP per capita evolution during the Spanish Flu was identical to the Great Recession until year 4. Specifically, the GDP regained the 2008 levels (1918) by 2011 (1921). After year 4, the evolution of the two shocks began to differ. In the Great Depression, GDP started to decline again by 2011, whereas the contrary happened in the 1918 influenza crisis since income continued growing after 1921. Specifically, GDP per capita decreased 6% between 2011 and 2015, and GDP per capita increased by 25% between 1921 and 1925. By the last available observation (2018), the GDP per capita was below the 2007 level. The decrease in GDP per capita was more profound during 1917 and 1921

Table 1.2 Global spread of the Spanish Flu

	Country	Death toll (absolute)	Death rate (per 1000)
America	Argentina	10,200	1.2
	Brazil	180,000	6.8
	Canada	50,000	6.1
	Mexico	300,000	20.6
	Uruguay	2,050	1.4
	United States	675,000	6.5
	Cameroon	250,000	44.5
Africa	Egypt	138,600	10.7
	Gambia	7,800	3.7
	Ghana	88,500	43.5
	Kenya	150,000	57.8
	Mauritius	12,000	31.8
	Nigeria	455,000	24.4
	South Africa	300,000	44.3
Asia	Sri Lanka	91,600	17.9
	China	4,000,000–9,500,000	8.4–20.1
	Indonesia	18,500,000	6.1
	Japan	388,000	7.0
	Philippines	93,686	1.7
	Taiwan	25,394	6.9
Europe	Austria	20,458	3.3
	Denmark	12,374	4.1
	Eire	18,367	4.3
	England and Wales	200,000	5.8
	Finland	18,000	5.8
	France	240,000	7.3
	Germany	225,330	3.8
	Hungary	100,000	12.7
	Italy	390,000	10.7
	Netherlands	48,042	7.1
	Norway	14,676	5.7
	Portugal	59,000	9.8
	Russia/USSR	450,000	2.4
	Scotland	27,650–33,771	5.7–6.9
	Spain	*245,046*	*12.2*
	Sweden	34,374	5.9
	Switzerland	23,277	6.1

Notes Data obtained from Johnson and Mueller (2002). Spanish data is from our estimates (Chapter 3)

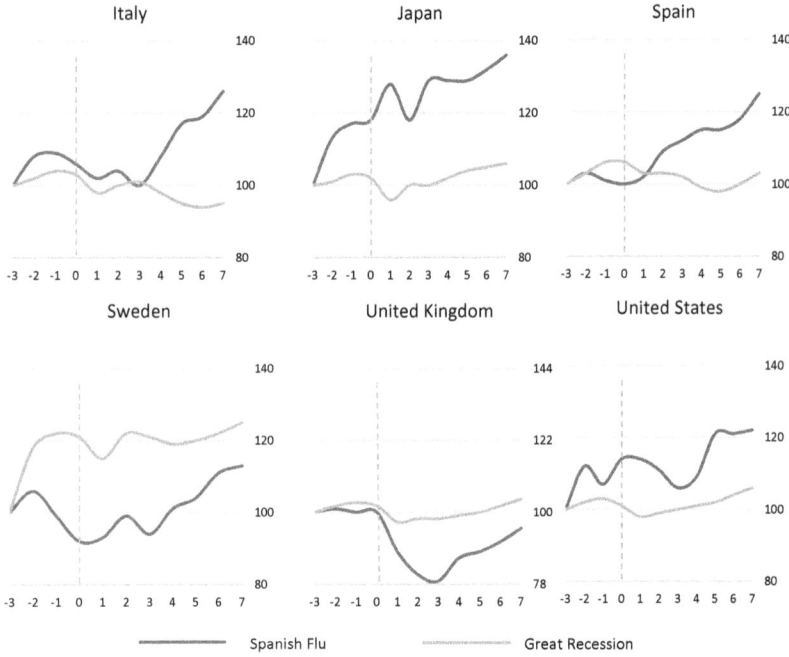

Fig. 1.1 The GDP shock of the Spanish Flu versus the Great Recession—selected countries (*Notes* year 0 is 1918 for the Spanish Flu [blue line] and 2008 for the Great Recession [orange line]. Real GDP per capita in 2011$. Data obtained from Madison Project Database [version 2020]. Bolt and van Zanden [2020])

(7%) than between 2007 and 2011 (3%). In sum, even though the output decline during the Spanish Flu was more severe than during the Great Recession, the Italian economy recovered faster during the Spanish Flu.[17] Lastly, we want to emphasize that the death rate during the Spanish Flu in Italy was one of the largest in Western Europe (see Table 1.2).

Japan. The Spanish Flu arrived in a moment of economic expansion. Indeed, between 1915 and 1918, real GDP per capita increased by 18%. This economic boom was briefly interrupted by a V-shaped recession during 1919–1920, with a decrease of 4% of the GDP per capita before economic growth restarted. In contrast, the country was already stagnant before the Great Recession. The GDP per capita decreased by 5%

in 2009 and slowly recovered afterwards, surpassing pre-shock levels four years later.

Spain. GDP per capita evolved differently before the Spanish Flu than before the Great Recession. Before the Spanish Flu, Spain was in a recession, which worsened in 1918. Therefore, GDP per capita reached its minimum in 1918 when the trend changed, and it experienced a rapid expansion during the 1920s due to rapid Total Factor Productivity (TFP) growth and investment (Prados de la Escosura and Rosés, 2009). For example, GDP per capita was 25% higher in 1925 than in 1918. In sharp contrast, the Spanish economy was booming before the Great Recession. After the shock, GDP per capita started to decline to reach a minimum by 2013. The subsequent recovery was incomplete since it had not regained the pre-shock level in 2018 (the last year in the dataset). The evolution in Spain is very similar to the Italian one in both economic crises, despite Spain's flu death rate being larger (see Table 1.2). The economic effects in Spain during the Spanish Flu, from which we hand-collected new data, will feature prominently in the rest of the book.

Sweden. The evolution of real GDP per capita in Sweden is like Spain, except during the recovery period after the Great Recession. The Swedish economy was in a recession when the Spanish Flu arrived. The minimum was in 1918, and the country boomed during the subsequent years, except for a brief decline in 1921. Before the Great Recession, the Swedish economy was also booming. After the crisis, the GDP stagnated, except during the 2009 contraction. The death rate in Sweden was almost half of the death rates in Italy and Spain. Sweden is one of the countries with more abundant literature on the Spanish Flu. We will review these findings throughout the book.

The United Kingdom. The evolution of GDP per capita in the United Kingdom after the shocks is the flipped side of the Italian one. British GDP was growing slowly before the two crises, but the economic reaction differed after each shock. After the Spanish Flu, the UK economy entered a deep recession. Between 1918 and 1921, GDP per capita declined 21%, and it did not recover the 1917 level until 1929. In comparison, the impact of the Great Recession was limited. From 2008 to 2011, GDP per capita declined 5%, and by 2015 the economy was again at the pre-crisis GDP level. The flu-related mortality rate in the United Kingdom is half the death rate of, for example, Spain (see Table 1.2). However, given that the United Kingdom did participate in World War I, its death toll must be interpreted cautiously. In any event, it is remarkable the substantial

British decline after the Great War. Unfortunately, the literature has not been able to disentangle how much is a consequence of the Spanish Flu and how much is the result of other factors or failed policies.

The United States. We will finish our list of selected countries with the United States. Before the Spanish Flu, the economy was booming. From 1915 to 1918, GDP per capita increased by 14%. However, GDP declined by 8% from 1918 to 1921, and most of World War I economic gains were lost. After 1921, the US economy boomed again. By 1925, GDP per capita was 22% higher than in 1915. The trend for the Great Recession is similar but flatter. In 1925, GDP per capita was 22% higher than in 1915. Instead, it was only 6% higher at the identical moment of the Great Recession. The death rate during the Spanish Flu was like the British one (half of the Spanish one). The economic effects of the Spanish Flu on the United States had received little attention until the emergence of Covid-19. The existing consensus before the Covid-19 was that tight monetary policy was the main culprit of the 1920 recession (see, for example, Friedman & Schwartz, 1963). We will discuss some recent empirical studies on the aggregate economic effects of the Spanish Flu in the United States in the last chapter of the book.

As a summary of Fig. 1.1, we want to emphasize three facts. First, the economic losses during the Spanish Flu were comparable in depth and length to the Great Recession. Therefore, the Spanish Flu was an economic depression, despite its economic impact has practically been ignored until the spread of Covid-19. Second, the economic consequences of the pandemic were extremely heterogeneous among different countries. Some countries grew during the episode, and others fell in a deep recession after 1918. In other words, it seems that the causal effects of the Spanish Flu are country dependent, and our knowledge could expand with country-case studies. Third, the death rate during the Spanish Flu does not seem a sufficient statistic to predict aggregate losses. Countries with roughly similar mortality rates experienced different economic paths. This evidence highlights the importance of country-case studies and casts doubts on studies that try to establish the economic behaviour of the "average" country during the pandemic.

To conclude, this section has discussed why the Spanish Flu was a dramatic pandemic. Moreover, it has also illustrated its negative impact on the economy as substantial as the recent Great Recession. However, despite its relevance, the Spanish Flu has remained as a footnote in most economic history books until the outburst of Covid-19 cases. In this sense, this book's goal is to provide a comprehensive and unified view of the effects of pandemics on the economy. We will discuss how the effects of the Spanish Flu may be different from other pandemics and how they may also be different across countries. To do so, we will use original data hand-collected by the authors for the Spanish economy and review the most recent academic research.

Plan of the Book

We finish this introductory chapter with a brief outline of the rest of the book. Chapter 2 describes the chronology of the Spanish Flu, and how the newspapers reported on the pandemic. In addition, we discuss how governments intervened to mitigate the death toll and economic losses. As we will see, these nonpharmaceutical interventions were very much akin to the ones used during the early stages of the Covid-19 pandemic, albeit full lockdown and curfews were scarcely employed during the 1918 influenza.

Chapter 3 analyses the unequal distribution of flu-related mortality within countries. First, we discuss the methodological complexities to assess flu-related mortality and how the task becomes even harder for belligerent countries. Then, we explain that flu-related mortality differed across ages, sex, occupations, and locations. One important lesson derived from our research for Spain is that climatic and socioeconomic disparities explain a substantial part of the spatial differences in flu-related mortality.

Chapter 4 considers the consequences of the pandemics on the labour market and wages. Wages are the most important indicator of overall welfare in the economy. First, we discuss the theoretical consequences of pre-industrialized world pandemics on wages and review the empirical literature. Then, we perform the analogous exercise for the Spanish Flu . Our main conclusion is that the Spanish flu reduced real wages. In that sense, we expect the Covid-19 to have, as we are observing, similar adverse effects on the labour market.

Chapter 5 is devoted to the pandemic effects on the capital market. Changes in the relative returns of capital affect inequality. One difficulty in this kind of exercise is that the asset composition of capital stocks has changed over time. During, for example, the Black Death, land was the most relevant asset and, hence, the main component of the capital stock.

In today's economies, housing is the most conspicuous asset and accounts for a large part of capital stock. Our conclusion from this chapter is that, beyond the effect on the relative assets' returns, the potential reallocation of capital across regions may be the most important long-term consequence of pandemics. Along these lines, we are currently observing how Covid-19 may be conducive to a reallocation of capital. Specifically, there has been an increase in housing demand in low-density areas, while the contrary can be observed in metropolitan areas.

The three previous chapters provide together a nuanced view of the effect of pandemics on well-being and income distribution. Many authors have considered that pandemics are "big levelers"[18] improving the lives of the less affluent members of society. The Spanish flu does not fit with that view. Our research shows that pandemic mortality was lower among the well-off classes, real wages decreased, and capital assets maintained or increased their value.

Finally, Chapter 6 explains the potential short- and long-run aggregate effects of pandemics. Even though there exists a consensus that pandemics (modern and past alike) have detrimental short-run effects, it is less clear the magnitude and direction of the long-run effects. As we will explain, economists have linked pandemics to both positive, negative, and null long-run effects on aggregate production. Therefore, we will finish the book without a straightforward prediction for the long-run consequences of Covid-19.

Notes

1. https://www.merriam-webster.com/dictionary/pandemic.
2. The identification of the Black Death as bubonic plague was subject to a long controversy. See, a review, in Theilmann and Cate (2007).
3. For more information, see, for example, Center for Disease Control and Prevention (CDC) website. https://www.cdc.gov/plague/transmission/index.html.
4. See, for example, Rosen (2007) or Scheidel (2017).
5. Mordechai et al. (2019).
6. The Spanish flu is also known as the Great Influenza epidemic or the 1918 influenza pandemic. In the period, it was also known as the "Spanish Lady".
7. Taubenberger and Morens (2006).
8. Cocolitztli means pest in Nathuati. This is a language of the Uto-Aztecan family and it is still spoken today.
9. Vagene et al. (2018).
10. This view is shared, for example, by Acuña-Soto et al. (2002), which examine the collapse in population in Mexico in the sixteenth century.

11. Acuña-Soto et al. (2002) provide information on the main waves of this demographic disaster. The first cocoliztli (1545–1548) killed between 5 and 15 million people (around 80% of the native population), and the second cocoliztli (1576–1578) claimed between 2 and 2.5 million people (about 50% of the remaining population).
12. For example, Collcutt (1987).
13. https://www.who.int/teams/global-hiv-hepatitis-and-stis-programmes/hiv/strategic-information/hiv-data-and-statistics.
14. https://www.who.int/data/gho/data/indicators/indicator-details/GHO/number-of-deaths-due-to-hiv-aids.
15. https://www.economist.com/leaders/2021/10/16/millions-of-lives-depend-on-how-the-pandemic-ends. We need to take this number with a grain of salt for, at least, two reasons. First, the pandemic is still ongoing and, thus, this number is bound to increase. Second, equally important, the methodology used by The Economist requires to make some assumptions because the data is not available for all countries. The Economist puts the global death toll between 10 and 19 million people.
16. Data of real GDP per capita (in 2011$) are obtained from Bolt and van Zanden (2020).
17. We do not want to make any causal inference. To begin with, Italy participated in World War I, which may have affected the post-war recovery. However, the uneven recovery of Italy after the two shocks may deserve further attention.
18. This concept is derived from Scheidel (2017).

References

Acuña-Soto, R., Stahle, D. W., Cleaveland, M. K., & Therrell, M. D. (2002). Megadrought and megadeath in 16th century Mexico. *Emerging Infectious Diseases, 8*(4), 360–362.

Bolt, J., & van Zanden, J. L. (2020). *Maddison style estimates of the evolution of the world economy. A new 2020 update* (Maddison-Project Working Paper WP-15).

Bowman, A. (2014). *Epidemics and mortality in early modern Japan*. Princeton University Press.

Bramanti, B., Dean, K. R., Walløe, L., & Stenseth, N. C. (2019). The third plague pandemic in Europe. *Proceedings of the Royal Society B: Biological Sciences, 286*(1901), 20182429.

Christakos, G., Olea, R., Serre, M., Yu, H., & Wang, L. (2005). *Interdisciplinary public health reasoning and epidemic modelling: The case of Black Death*. Springer.

Cirillo, P., & Taleb, N. N. (2020). Tail risk of contagious diseases. *Nature Physics, 16*, 606–613.
Collcutt, M. (1987). Review "population, disease, and land in early Japan, 645–900 William Wayne Farris." *Harvard Journal of Asiatic Studies, 47*(1), 299–310.
Farris, W. W. (2020). *Population, disease, and land in early Japan, 645-900*. Brill.
Fortson, J. G. (2011). Mortality risk and human capital investment: The impact of HIV/AIDS in Sub-Saharan Africa. *Review of Economics and Statistics, 93*(1), 1–15.
Friedman, M., & Schwartz, A. (1963). *A monetary history of the United States (1867–1960)*. Princeton University Press.
Jedwab, R., Johnson, N., & Koyama, M. (2021). The economic impact of the Black Death. *Journal of Economic Literature*, forthcoming.
Johnson, N., & Mueller, J. (2002). Updating the accounts: Global mortality of the 1918–1920 "Spanish" influenza pandemic. *Bulletin of the History of Medicine, 76*, 105–115.
Jones, C. I., & Klenow, P. J. (2016). Beyond GDP? Welfare across countries and time. *American Economic Review, 106*(9), 2426–2457.
Kalemli-Ozcan, S., & Turan, B. (2011). HIV and fertility revisited. *Journal of Development Economics, 96*(1), 61–65.
Mordechai, L., Eisenberg, M., Newfield, T. P., Izdebski, A., Kay, J. E., & Poinar, H. (2019). The Justinianic Plague: An inconsequential pandemic? *Proceedings of the National Academy of Sciences, 116*(51), 25546–25554.
Prados de la Escosura, L., & Rosés, J. R. (2009). The sources of long-run growth in Spain, 1850–2000. *Journal of Economic History, 69*(4), 1063–1091.
Prem, H. (1991). Disease outbreaks in Central Mexico during the sixteenth century. In N. D. Cook & G. W. Lovello (Eds.), *Secret Judgments of God: Old World Disease in Colonial Spanish America* (pp. 20–48). Norman.
Rosen, W. (2007). *Justinian's Flea: The First Great Plague and the End of the Roman Empire*. Penguin.
Scheidel, W. (2017). *The great leveler: Violence and the history of inequality from the stone age to the twenty-first century*. Princeton University Press.
Taubenberger, J. K., & Morens, D. (2006). 1918 influenza: The mother of all pandemics. *Emerging Infectious Diseases, 12*(1), 15–22.
Theilmann, J., & Cate, F. (2007). A plague of plagues: The problem of plague diagnosis in medieval England. *Journal of Interdisciplinary History, 37*(3), 371–393.
Vågene, Å. J., Herbig, A., Campana, M. G., Robles García, N. M., Warinner, C., Sabin, S., Spyrou, M. A., Andrades Valtueña, A., Huson, D., Tuross, N., Bos, K. I., & Krause, J. (2018). Salmonella enterica genomes from victims of a major sixteenth-century epidemic in Mexico. *Nature Ecology & Evolution, 2*(3), 520–528.
Young, A. (2005). The gift of the dying: The tragedy of aids and the welfare of future African generations. *Quarterly Journal of Economics, 120*(2), 423–466.

CHAPTER 2

The Spanish Flu: A Global Shock

Abstract As Covid-19, the Spanish Flu was a global pandemic, hitting countries at roughly similar times. However, there were substantial differences in mortality rates between and within countries. The Spanish Flu spread across the world through the movements of troops in the Great War, international trade networks, and migrant flows. The pandemic expanded typically in three subsequent waves: the initial wave of the summer of 1918; the deadliest wave during the autumn of 1918; and a third, milder one, during the subsequent winter. There were some differences in the timing of the emergence of the first news about the pandemic. However, by the peak month of October 1918, the European and North American population was aware of the relevance of this deadly pandemic. Outside Europe and North America, pandemic news circulated much more slowly or perhaps not at all. To respond to the pandemic, nonpharmaceutical government interventions were put in pace.

Keywords Pandemic diffusion · Newspapers · Nonpharmacological interventions

© The Author(s), under exclusive license to Springer Nature Switzerland AG 2022
S. Basco et al., *Pandemics, Economics and Inequality*,
Palgrave Studies in Economic History,
https://doi.org/10.1007/978-3-031-05668-0_2

Origins and Chronology of the Pandemic

Although phylogenetic analyses failed to place the origins of the virus in any region of the world,[1] the first recorded case of an outbreak of H1N1 influenza was in Haskell County, Kansas, later spreading to the US army's Camp Funston.[2] Alternative views are that the origin of the pandemic began in a hospital camp in Étaples (France) in late 1917[3] or China.[4] In any case, as we mentioned in Chapter 1, the first outbreak of the great influenza pandemic was not in Spain.

A substantial Spanish Flu literature argues the existence of three waves in this pandemic in Europe and in the United States: a first wave, the "herald" one, during the summer of 1918; a second one in the autumn of 1918, and a third, milder one, during the winter 1918/1919.[5]

The initial spread of the pandemic took place in the United States and the Allied European countries during the summer of 1918.[6] This initial pandemic wave was also present outside this core group affecting neutral countries, like Sweden, Denmark, the Netherlands, and Switzerland, and Entente countries, like Germany, albeit with some delay. The pandemic reached Russia in two ways: throughout the western border in late August and carried out by the Allies army through the ports of Murmansk and Arkhangelsk in early September.[7]

This "herald" wave of this pandemic was also present in other continents. China experienced the first mild wave of the pandemic by June–July 1918. It involved at least three major cities (Beijing, Tianjin, Shanghai) and more than 14 provinces, including Heilongjiang, Jilin, Jiangsu, Zhejiang, Anhui, and Guangdong. In India, the first reported cases of the Spanish flu were in Bombay in June 1918. In Indonesia, the pandemic arrived at the town of Pankattan on the east coast of Sumatra in June 1918. The influenza epidemic entered Iran via the western border in June–July 1918. In May and June 1918, the Spanish flu was also present in Algeria and Egypt. Mild initial flu waves happened in several Latin American countries, including Mexico, Peru, and Chile but not in Colombia or Brazil. Other countries that escaped to this first wave were Japan, Taiwan, and Australia.[8]

One potential transmission channel of the first pandemic wave might have been new soldiers' movements from the United States to Western European trenches in 1918. However, the pandemic also voyaged with the international trade networks and migrations to the non-belligerent countries. The Allied and Entente authorities censored pandemic news to protect morale during World War I[9] and, hence, the population was not generally aware of the existence of the pandemic until autumn 1918.

The second wave was the deadliest one. Typically, this took place during the autumn of 1918 and was practically universal. Some literature argues that the pandemic virus during the first wave had conferred substantial protection during the second wave (Simonsen et al., 2018). In the countries that avoided the "herald" wave, this wave had different behaviour. In Japan, the wave lasted longer than in other countries from October 1918 to May 1919 and in Australia did not emerge until January 1919. Finally, other countries outside the "core" of the pandemic had also different chronologies. For example, the pandemic was at its most virulent in Chile in July–August 1919.[10]

The variation within countries was also considerable, even with the timing of the waves. In the United States , pneumonia and influenza death rates varied from around 5 per 1,000 to 11.2 per 1000 (Brainerd & Siegler, 2003). In Sweden, 16 out of 26 counties had lower mortality than expected in 1918–1919, whereas the remaining ten counties had mortality rates well above the historical time trends. In Chile, the overall mortality rate was 9.4 per thousand, but rates could vary by one order of magnitude in the different provinces. In India, the pandemic hit the west of India first and peaked later in the East.[11]

Figure 2.1 records pandemic excess mortality rates in Spain.[12] Spain also experienced the three pandemic waves,[13] but these are substantially different to the English and Wales ones (Pearce et al., 2011, Figure 1).[14] This first wave lasted until July. There was a small death peak in June of 1918, with excess mortality of around 30%. The most affected zone was the province of Madrid and some provinces in South Castile and Andalusia.[15] One popular view is that the virus reached Spain with temporary workers returning from France to their provinces of origin. However, it is unclear if the timing of these flows of workers correlated with the 1918 wave. There was also the movement of Portuguese troops crossing the north of Spain in railroad cars and seasonal migrations from Portugal (Trilla et al., 2008).

The second wave started in September and lasted until December. The excess mortality rate during October was impressive (347%). This number implies that the number of deaths in October 1918 were 4.47 times larger than in a normal October. In November, excess deaths decreased but they still represented more than twice the number of deaths of a typical November (169% increase). There is no sight of the third wave in the coming winter months of 1918/1919. In January of 1920, there was a

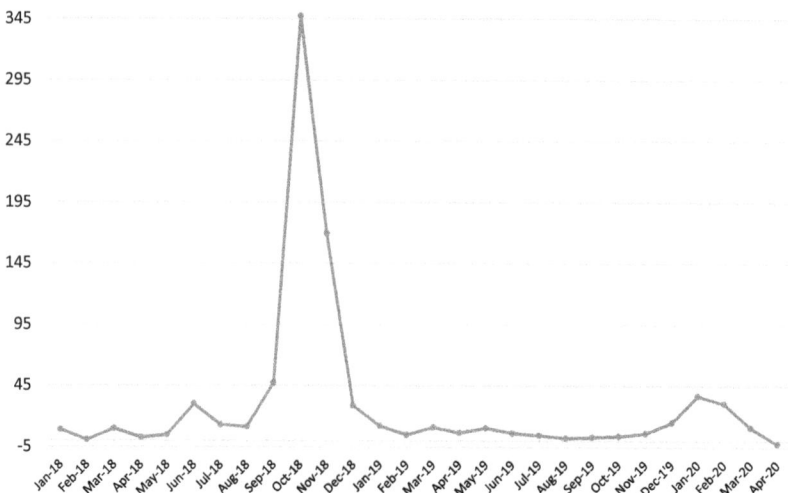

Fig. 2.1 Evolution of flu-related excess mortality in Spain, January 1918–April 1920 (*Notes* The source of the underlining demographic data is Historical database of the Spanish National Institute of Statistics [INE], *Movimiento natural de la población* [https://www.ine.es/inebase_historia/mnp.htm]. See the main text for more information on the definition of excess mortality and the calculations)

slight increase in mortality but weaker compared with the previous two. A plausible explanation for the small significant third wave in Spain is that the fall wave was so intense and the exposure so widespread that inhabitants gained immune protection.[16]

SPANISH FLU IN THE NEWS

Newspapers reported the initial wave in different countries during the spring of 1918. The reported symptoms were similar. Spanish newspapers started reporting news about a new influenza epidemic in May 1918, when the virulence of the October 1918 outbreak was impossible to predict. El *Porvenir Castellano*, a newspaper from Northern Castile, on 13th May 1918 announced that in Dueñas (province of Palencia), there were more than 200 influenza cases and that the local authorities had taken measures to stop the spread of the epidemic.

On 22nd May 1918, the influenza epidemic was a headline in Madrid's *ABC* newspaper. Despite the rapid diffusion of the new infection, the newspaper insisted that the unknown illness was mild and with ordinary influenza-like symptoms. This illness presented gastrointestinal symptoms, 2- or 3-days fever, and general malaise. Also, it was associated with a low mortality rate (Trilla et al., 2008). On the same day, Barcelona's *La Vanguardia* reported a comment by the famous doctor Gregorio Marañón on the evolution of the pandemic in Madrid. The knowledge of doctor Marañón seems to be pretty accurate. He pointed out that something like "grippe" or influenza, with air transmission, caused the epidemic. He also argued that atmospheric and weather changes were responsible for the explosiveness of the pandemic in Madrid. Lastly, he recommended avoiding crowded indoor spaces. Despite the soothing words of doctor Marañón, the *Diario de Alicante* declared on the same day that: "The current epidemic takes scary proportions. Until now, the disease has not caused any death. The alarm is gigantic. Public institutions have many members on sick leave".

The epidemic was expanding quickly in Madrid, and the public and newspapers were worried. For example, *El Progreso*, a newspaper from Lugo, reported on 23rd May 1918: "Flu epidemic in the royal entourage confirmed. In theatres and other establishments, there are hundreds of infections (…) the epidemic is markedly benign". Similarly, Madrid's *La Correspondencia de España* declared on 23rd May 1918 that in the Spanish capital: "The epidemic, which is not serious, but annoying, has now invaded thousands of people and there is no family in Madrid, no public institution, no theatre or factory without at least a member on sick leave…". In late spring of 1918, the Spanish press agency Fabra reported to Reuters that "A strange form of the disease of epidemic character has appeared in Madrid. The epidemic is of a mild nature, with no deaths reported" (Trilla et al., 2008).

Basco et al. (2021) computes the evolution of *La Vanguardia*'s news and ads that mentioned the words "grippe" (the name of the flu in Spain) or influenza. Despite being printed in Barcelona, this newspaper has detailed coverage of news across Spain, which occupied a substantial part of the newspaper. In other words, this newspaper is representative of the spread of the pandemic news across Spanish provinces.

Figure 2.2 reports the evolution of pandemic news. The monthly data begins in January 1918 and finishes in April 1920. The number of hits started to increase in April 1918. It reached a peak in June 1918, when

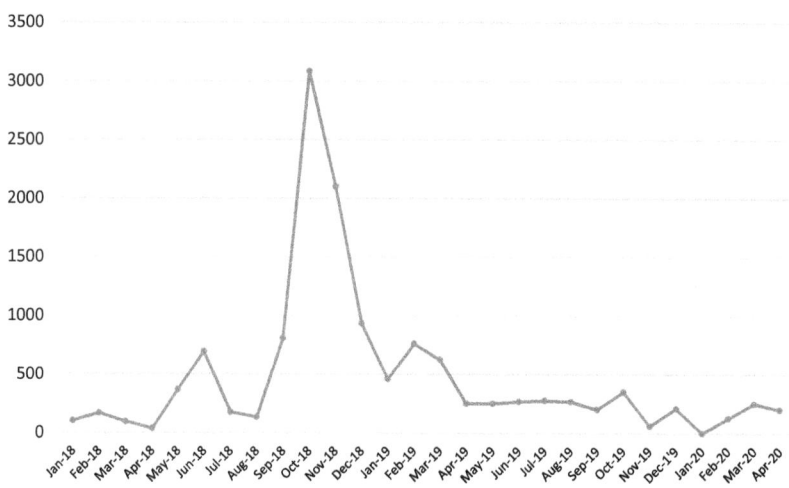

Fig. 2.2 Evolution of flu-related mentions in Spanish newspapers, January 1918–April 1920 (*Notes* Index of "epidemic" and "grippe" mentions in *La Vanguardia from* January 1918 to April 1920. January 1918 = 100. *Source* https://www.lavanguardia.com/hemeroteca)

influenza infections were already visible, especially in Madrid. The number of hits in June was seven times larger than in January. After this first news wave, the pandemic mentions decreased quickly. By August 1918, the number of hits was like January. Pandemic mentions went up again in September 1918, exploding in the next month. The number of flu-related hits in October 1918 was 31 times larger than in January 1918. After October, it decreased quickly. In January 1919, the number of flu-related hits was around five times the level in the same month of 1918. Another smaller peak took place in February 1919, with 7.5 times the mentions of earlier 1918.

The trend in flu mentions in *La Vanguardia* is also clearly observable in other Spanish newspapers. Basco et al. (2021) check the flu mentions in Madrid's ABC. In this newspaper, the highest interest in influenza was between September 1918 and March 1919, peaking in October 1918. One can obtain a similar result with a search of the pandemic's words ("grippe" or "gripe") in the digitized Spanish newspapers collection.[17] From 1st April 1918 to 31st March 1920, the searches yield 17,492 hits in over 150 newspapers. The number of hits is the highest from September 1918 to March 1919, peaking in October 1918.

The timing of Spain's news closely matched the unfolding of the pandemic in the Western countries, including Spain. In belligerent countries, however, some lags are apparent in newspaper hits. We have replicated the previous exercise using digitized British newspapers located in the *British Newspaper Archive* (Fig. 2.3). Characteristically, the news on the pandemic had a lag of one or two months. There were not much news of the flu during the first wave of May 1918, except in July. Later, as pandemic-related deaths grew exponentially in October, the increase in influenza-related hits was particularly acute in November 1918. In contrast, Spanish newspapers reported infectious outbreaks and flu-related deaths by September.[18]

It is also interesting to compare the news intensity and the pandemic chronology between British and Spanish newspapers. Regarding the news intensity, the highest peak in Spanish newspapers by October 1918 had 31 times more hits than in January 1918. Instead, the highest peak in British newspapers by November 1918 had only 13 times more hits

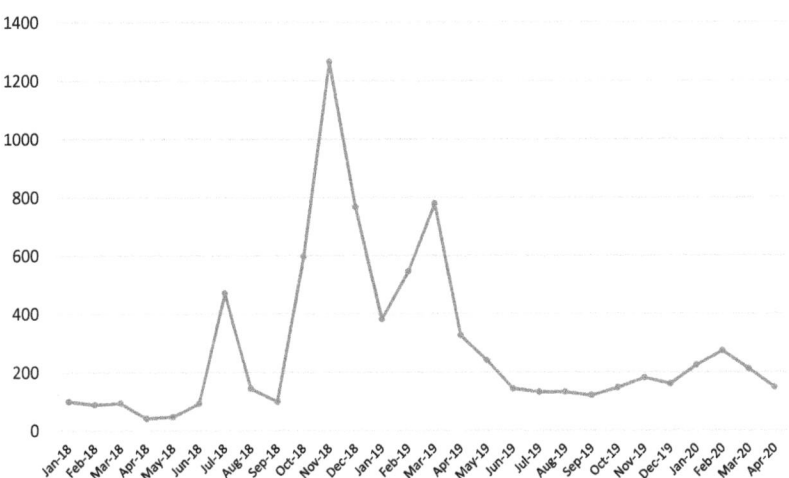

Fig. 2.3 Evolution of "influenza" News in British newspapers, January 1918–April 1920 (*Notes* Index of mentions of "influenza" in *British Newspapers from January 1918 to April 1920*. January 1918 = 100. https://www.britishnewspaperarchive.co.uk/search/advanced)

than the initial value. One can also identify three waves in the evolution of the number of hits in British newspapers. The first wave was in the summer of 1918, with a peak in July. The second wave, also the largest one, was in autumn 1918, with the maximum number of hits in November. And the third one in winter 1919, with a peak in March. Instead, the presence of these three waves is unclear in the Spanish data. For example, in British newspapers, the number of hints in the winter 1919 peak was around 60% of the fall peak. In Spanish newspapers, it was only 24%. One can hypothesize that these differences in news waves were the direct consequence of differences in mortality trends between these two countries.

We next turn to the spread of pandemic news in the United States. Like British newspapers, the *New York Times* published sparse pandemic news before October. There were only two mentions of influenza in the Army by March 1918. However, the newspaper published the following information on 5th April 1918: "Army Health continues good". The New York Times information on the Pandemic was akin to war propaganda during the summer months. For example, it said, "spread of disease described sailor tailor, who says Spanish epidemic came from Germany and that other countries will likewise be affected" (21st June 1918). On 27th June, its reporters wrote: "Spanish Influenza is Raging in the German Army". And, on 14th July, they also wrote: "Germans Die of Hunger; malady described as influenza is really due to starvation". The tone of the reports changed during the autumn, and the newspapers began to recognize the importance of the pandemic in the United States. So, they noted that "FD Roosevelt Spanish grip victim" (20th September 1918) and "Baltimore lacks coffins" (19th October 1918).

The *New York Times* also published news on the worldwide expansion of the Pandemic during the autumn of 1918. On 19th October 1918, the newspaper informed: "Influenza in West Africa: 1,000 deaths a week in Sierra Leone". The next day, the news was: "Jamaica has now epidemic" and "Canada in grip of epidemic". On 23rd October 1918, it published "disease spreads in Argentina" and two days later: "Influenza in Copenhagen: mortality is high and there is scarcity of drugs". Finally, on 28th October 1918, it published, "Epidemic delays coffee shipments. Influenza delays shipments from Brazil".

Public Interventions

The available evidence on nonpharmaceutical interventions from the authorities during the pandemic comes mainly from the United States. Markel et al. (2007) classify those measures into three categories: (i) school closures, (ii) public gathering bans, and (iii) isolation and quarantine of confirmed and suspected cases.[19] On some occasions, interventions went as far as closing non-essential businesses. The authorities implemented the earliest measures in mid-September 1918, but some cities and states did not enact their interventions until mid-October. There was a considerable variation across places on the implementation, type of measures, and duration. The extent of these interventions was generally short since they had an average time of only around one month. Therefore, many authorities lifted restrictions before the third wave arrived by January 1919.

The main question is whether these nonpharmaceutical interventions were sufficient and efficient. Crosby (2003) forcefully argues that the electing representatives had to decide among three competing issues: national security (the country was at war), economic growth, and public health. In broad terms, they opted to protect the first two and, hence, undermined the containing of the pandemic. Therefore, interventions were, in general, hesitant and limited in scope and time.

Regarding their impact on mortality, Bootsma and Ferguson (2007) calculate that they reduced mortality by about 10–30% during the second wave. They also point out that authorities implemented many interventions too late and lifted them earlier than was necessary to protect the population.[20] These nonpharmaceutical interventions helped flatten the curve in the sense of reducing the peak deaths to average deaths, but the effect on overall deaths was small and statistically insignificant because they were too limited in time. Barro (2020) recently re-examines the previous findings. He also finds that the impact on the relative peak death rate of nonpharmaceutical interventions is negative and statistically significant, and their influence on the cumulative death rate is negative but not significant.

An interesting counterfactual to the limited life-saving impact of these interventions comes from the locations that implemented the most stringent measures. In this sense, Crosby (2003) shows that cities with less mortality introduced measures early and kept them in place after the second wave. Similarly, Markel et al. (2007) underline that the seven cities with less flu mortality implemented early isolation or "protective sequestration".

There were strong parallelisms between Spanish nonpharmaceutical interventions and those implemented in the United States. Despite not being belligerent during the Great War, the Spanish health authorities opted to protect the economy over the health of the citizens. Like in the United States, decisions on implementing nonpharmaceutical interventions were taken by a decentralized institution. In each province, the prefect (the highest government political authority) and the health commission ("Junta Provincial Sanitaria") could officially declare the existence of a pandemic and implement different measures. Sometimes, the decisions were controversial and contested by local businesses and even the Church (Trilla et al., 2008). Consequently, in many situations, policies were implemented later and lasted less time than was necessary. The Spanish newspapers also reported, with substantial detail, the measures taken by the authorities to control the pandemic.

In many towns and cities in Spain, authorities recommended that sick patients were isolated, forbid large gatherings (for example, local festivities, religious parades, theatres, music, and dance halls were closed), and closed primary and high schools as well as universities. Military conscription was provisionally halted to avoid the movement of new conscripts from one province to another. In prisons, sick prisoners were isolated and given medical treatment. However, in late September, many theatres and concert halls were open, and, in most cases, they were very crowded (29th September 1918, *La Vanguardia*). It is important to emphasize that there is no evidence of strict lockdowns and closing of establishments, workshops, and stores (except when all their workers were sick) enforced by authorities. Similarly, harvests took place since we cannot observe a decrease in agricultural production.[21] In sum, self-isolation was a personal decision neither imposed nor supported with grants by the authorities.

The contemporary understanding of contagion channels was reasonably accurate. The measures taken denote some accumulated knowledge of dealing with epidemics, especially in urban settings.[22] However, in the Mediterranean countries, some of the implemented hygienic measures were not effective since they were akin to those employed during recent cholera outbreaks. Therefore, Spanish authorities combined the universal recommendations of avoiding crowded, poorly ventilated spaces and multitudes with the widespread use of disinfectant, the washing of fruits and vegetables, and the cleaning of public toilets.[23] Councils also gave substantial publicity to these cleaning measures to tranquillize the public (Basco et al., 2021).[24] There is also very little evidence that masks were used in Spain, despite the international recommendation for their use. In contrast, in the United States or Japan there was widespread usage.[25]

The response of the Spanish health system was completely inadequate. Some rural zones lacked medical assistance and when physicians died, they were difficult to replace. Furthermore, the different treatments failed, even some experimental vaccines were also tried (Trilla et al., 2008).

A Global Shock with Local Effects

Despite the fast diffusion of the pandemic, there are surprising differences in mortality rates between countries and within countries themselves. The reasons for these differences are poorly understood. The adoption and enforcement of nonpharmacological interventions varied across locations and countries. Disease knowledge as well. Self-isolation and quarantines were more likely in affluent countries than in the poorer ones. Everywhere, the rich had more means to isolate themselves and avoid social interactions. Finally, the previous history of related diseases implies that several cohorts typically could have more protection from the virus.[26]

In Table 1.2 in Chapter 1, we reported the estimates of flu-related deaths collected by Johnson and Mueller (2002). The authors recognize that the reporting of influenza-related deaths could be significantly underestimated. We present these numbers because they provide a global picture of the differences in flu impact. Despite the potential underestimation, less developed areas in Europe, Africa, Asia, or America had much higher mortality rates than in North-Western Europe and North America. In Central and Southern Europe, mortality rates almost doubled North-Western Europe. In America, Guatemala and Mexico had mortality rates that were several times the mortality rates in the United States or Canada. Similarly, in Asia, the mortality rate estimate for Indonesia is also more than three times higher than the mortality rates in Western European countries. African estimates are also much higher, with Cameroon getting an improbably high number, close to 50% mortality rate, Egypt had the lowest, similarly to the high end of experiences in Europe, but all the other countries have much higher rates.

The margins of error for the poorest regions of the world are substantial. Furthermore, we are not sure about the direction of the bias. In Indonesia, previous accounts underestimated death rates. The traditional estimate was only 1.5 million deaths. However, only in Java, Chandra (2014) estimates 4.26 to 4.37 million flu-related deaths. On the contrary, for India, the early assumptions of Davis (1951) were off the mark. Chandra et al. (2012) reduce the estimates of flu-related deaths from 17–18 million to 13.88 million. Using better population data, Chandra (2013) also documents that mortality rates were much lower in Japan, at around 3.7%, than was before calculated.

To conclude, we have seen massive mortality differences between and within countries during the pandemic. These mortality differences may be related to the quality of institutions, level of development, wealth, and available information, which will also likely determine the economic impact. Thus, it seems clear that even though the Spanish Flu was a global shock, the economic effects were local.

Notes

1. Taubenberger and Morens (2006).
2. Barry (2004), and Barry et al. (2008).
3. Oxford et al. (2005).
4. Shortridge (1999) and Spinney (2017).
5. See, for example, Simonsen et al. (2018) and Taubenberger and Morens (2006).
6. Chowell et al. (2008) and Simonsen et al. (2018).
7. See Simonsen et al. (2018) for the Entente Countries; and Morozova et al. (2021) on Russia.
8. See Wu (2020) on China; Singh (2021) on India; Gallardo-Albarrán and de Zwart (2021) on Indonesia; Azizi et al. (2010) on Iran; Simonsen et al. (2018) on Algeria, Taiwan and the Latin American countries; Rose (2021) on Egypt; Rice and Palmer (1993), and Richard et al. (2009) on Japan; and Shaw (2020) on Australia.
9. Barry (2004), Collier (1996), and Kolata (1999).
10. See, Rice and Palmer (1993) and Richard et al. (2009) about Japan; Shaw (2020) on Australia; and Chowell et al. (2014) on Chile.
11. See, Karlsson et al. (2014) on Sweden; Chowell et al. (2014) on Chile: and Chandra and Kassens-Noor (2014) on India.
12. See Chapter 3 for a full discussion on this mortality measure.
13. Echeverri (1985) and Chowell et al. (2014) also claim the presence of three waves in the flu in Spain. Cilek et al. (2018) detect three waves, but their results are circumscribed to the city of Madrid.

14. In England and Wales, the first wave during summer 1918 had a mortality of 0.03%, the autumn wave was the most severe with a mortality rate of 0.27%, and the third (winter) wave was less severe, with an average mortality of 0.1%. Therefore, the autumn wave concentrated about two-thirds of the total deaths (Pearce et al., 2011).
15. Chowell et al. (2014), Table 2.
16. On the issue of immune protection due to the previous diffusion of the virus, see, among others, Barry et al. (2008), Pierce et al. (2011) and Simonsen et al. (2018).
17. The collection comprises newspapers from all Spanish provinces, and it is curated by the Spain's Ministry of Culture and Sports. https://prensahistorica.mcu.es/es/inicio/inicio.do.
18. For instance, *La Vanguardia*, on 19th September 1918, reported "The province hardest hit by the pandemic is Huesca, because of its proximity with the frontier (with France, n,.a.). In the town of Alpiés there are 280 infected, of which 10 have already died, apparently because of influenza. (…) In the town of Lanuza, an individual had just got back from France, the disease attacked him, later dying." Similarly, on 20th September 1918, reporting from the Spanish province of Logroño it read "We receive communication from Briones of 80 infections and 4 deaths". On the 29th of September it reported "In the Córdoba regiment there are 82 (flu) infections, 4 soldiers have died."
19. Similar data have been also collected by Crosby (2003), Hatchett et al. (2007), and Bootsma and Ferguson (2007). More recently, Berkes et al. (2020) have increased the size of the sample by adding several new cities.
20. Markel et al. (2007) shares a similar view.
21. See, Chapter 6.
22. Rodríguez Ocaña (1994) and Pérez Moreda et al. (2015).
23. Tognotti (2003) and Trilla et al. (2008).
24. These cleaning measures included sometimes the killing of all the street dogs, as they did in the city of Bilbao (*La Vanguardia*, 8th October 1918).
25. At the height of the pandemic in the West of England, doctors, and nurses "attending to influenza patients should wear an improvised face mask", of "16 by 6 inches, stretch across face, cut a vertical slit of about 2 inches long on each side to hitch over ears" (11th November 1918, *Western Daily Press*). On 25th October 1918, wearing masks was made compulsory in San Francisco: "Board of Supervisors passes ordinance compelling every person to wear gauze mask." (*New York Times*).
26. A full discussion of the causes of these differences is the matter of the following chapter.

References

Azizi, M. H., Raees, G. H., & Azizi, F. (2010). A history of the 1918 Spanish influenza pandemic and its impact on Iran. *Archives of Iranian Medicine*, 13(3), 262–265.

Barry, J. M. (2004). *The great influenza: The story of the deadliest pandemic in history*. Penguin.

Barry, J. M., Viboud, C., & Simonsen, L. (2008). Cross-protection between successive waves of the 1918–1919 influenza pandemic: Epidemiological evidence from US Army camps and from Britain. *Journal of Infectious Diseases*, 198(10), 1427e34.

Barro, R., Ursúa, J., & Weng, J. (2020). *The coronavirus and the great influenza pandemic. Lessons from the "Spanish Flu" for the coronavirus's potential effects on mortality and economic activity* (NBER Working Papers 26866).

Basco, S., Domènech, J., & Rosés, J. R. (2021). *Unequal Mortality during the Spanish Flu* (CEPR Discussion Papers, 15783).

Berkes, E., Deschenes, O., Gaetani, R., Lin, J., & Severen, C. (2020). *Lockdowns and innovation: Evidence from the 1918 flu pandemic* (NBER Working Papers, w28152).

Bootsma, M. C. J., & Ferguson, N. M. (2007). Public health interventions and epidemic intensity during the 1918 influenza pandemic. *Proceedings of the National Academy of Sciences*, 104(18), 7588–7593.

Brainerd, E., & Siegler, M. (2003). *The economic effects of the 1918 influenza pandemic* (CEPR Discussion Papers, 3791).

Chandra, S. (2013). Deaths associated with influenza pandemic of 1918–19 Japan. *Emerging Infectious Diseases*, 19(4), 616–622.

Chandra, S. (2014). Mortality from the influenza pandemic of 1918–1919 in Indonesia. *Population Studies*, 67(2), 185–193.

Chandra, S. and Kassens-Noor, E. (2014). The evolution of the pandemic influenza: evidence from India, 1918–1919. *BMC Infectious diseases*, 14 (510).

Chandra, S., Kuljanin, G., & Way, J. (2012). Mortality from the pandemic of 1918–1919: The case of India. *Demography*, 49(3), 857–865.

Chowell, G., Bettencourt, L. M., Johnson, N., Alonso, W. J., & Viboud, C. (2008). The 1918–1919 influenza pandemic in England and Wales: Spatial patterns in transmissibility and mortality impact. *Proceedings of the Royal Society B: Biological Sciences*, 275(1634), 501–509.

Chowell, G., Erkoreka, A., Viboud, C., & Echeverri-Dávila, B. (2014). Spatial-temporal excess mortality patterns of the 1918–1919 influenza pandemic in Spain. *BMC Infectious Diseases*, 14, 371.

Cilek, L., Chowell, G., & Ramiro Fariñas, D. (2018). Age-specific excess mortality patterns during the 1918–1920 influenza pandemic in Madrid Spain. *American Journal of Epidemiology*, 187(12), 2511–2523.

Collier, R. (1996). *The plague of the Spanish Lady*. Allison and Busby.
Crosby, A. W. (2003). *America's forgotten pandemic: The influenza of 1918*. Cambridge University Press.
Davis, K. (1951). *The population of India and Pakistan*. Princeton University Press.
Echeverrri, B. (1985). *La gripe Española. La pandemia de 1918–1919*. Centro de Investigaciones Sociológicas (CIS).
Gallardo-Albarrán, D., & Zwart, P. (2021). A bitter epidemic: The impact of the 1918 influenza on sugar production in Java. *Economics and Human Biology*, 42, 101011.
Hatchett, R. J., Mecher, C. E., & Lipsitch, M. (2007). Public health interventions and epidemic intensity during the 1918 influenza pandemic. *Proceedings of the National Academy of Sciences*, 104(18), 7582–7587.
Johnson, N., & Mueller, J. (2002). Updating the accounts: Global mortality of the 1918–1920 "Spanish" influenza pandemic. *Bulletin of the History of Medicine*, 76, 105–115.
Karlsson, M., Nilsson, T., & Pichler, S. (2014). The impact of the 1918 Spanish flu epidemic on economic performance in Sweden: An investigation into the consequences of an extraordinary mortality shock. *Journal of Health Economics*, 36(1), 1–19.
Kolata, G. (1999). *Flu: The story of the great influenza pandemic of 1918 and the search for the virus that caused it*. Simon and Schuster.
Markel, H., Lipman, H. B., Navarro, J. A., Sloan, A., Michalsen, J. R., Stern, A. M., & Cetron, M. S. (2007). Nonpharmaceutical interventions implemented by US cities during the 1918–1919 influenza pandemic. *JAMA*, 298(6), 644–654.
Morozova, O. M., Troshina, T. I., Morozova, E. N., & Morozov, A. N. (2021). The Spanish flu pandemic in 1918 in Russia. Questions a hundred years later. *Journal of Microbiology, Epidemiology and Immunobiology*, 98(1), 113–124.
Oxford, J. S., Lambkin, R., Sefton, A., Daniels, R., Elliot, A., Brown, R., & Gill, D. (2005). A hypothesis: The conjunction of soldiers, gas, pigs, ducks, geese and horses in Northern France during the Great War provided the conditions for the emergence of the "Spanish" influenza pandemic of 1918–1919. *Vaccine*, 23(7), 940–945.
Pearce, D. C., Pallaghy, P. K., McCaw, J. M., McVernon, J., & Mathews, J. D. (2011). Understanding mortality in the 1918–1919 influenza pandemic in England and Wales. *Influenza and Other Respiratory Viruses*, 5(2), 89–98.
Pérez Moreda, V., Reher, D. S., & Gimeno, A. S. (2015). La conquista de la salud: Mortalidad y modernización en la España contemporánea. *Madrid*, 75, 87–110.

Rice, G. W., & Palmer, E. (1993). Pandemic influenza in Japan, 1918-19: Mortality patterns and official responses. *Journal of Japanese Studies, 19*(2), 389–420.

Richard, S. A., Sugaya, N., Simonsen, L., Miller, M. A., & Viboud, C. (2009). A comparative study of the 1918-1920 influenza pandemic in Japan, USA and UK: mortality impact and implications for pandemic planning. *Epidemiology and Infection, 137*(8), 1062e72.

Rose, C. S. (2021). Implications of the Spanish influenza pandemic (1918-1920) for the history of early 20th century Egypt. *Journal of World History, 32*(4), 655–684.

Rodríguez Ocaña, E. (1994). La Salud Pública en España en el contexto europeo, 1890-1925. *Revista de Sanidad e Higiene Pública, 68*, 11–27.

Shaw, I. W. (2020). *Pandemic: The Spanish Flu in Australia 1918–20.* Woodslane Press.

Shortridge, K. F. (1999). The 1918 'Spanish' flu: Pearls from swine? *Nature Medicine, 5*(4), 384–385.

Simonsen, L., Chowell, G., Andreasen, V., Gaffey, R., Barry, J., Olson, D., & Viboud, C. (2018). A review of the 1918 herald pandemic wave: Importance for contemporary pandemic response strategies. *Annals of Epidemiology, 28*(5), 281–288.

Singh, M. (2021). Bombay Fever/Spanish Flu: Public health and native press in Colonial Bombay, 1918-19. *South Asia Research, 41*(1), 35–52.

Spinney, L. (2017). *Pale rider: The Spanish flu of 1918 and how it changed the world.* Public Affairs.

Taubenberger, J. K., & Morens, D. (2006). 1918 influenza: The mother of all pandemics. *Emerging Infectious Diseases, 12*(1), 15–22.

Tognotti, E. (2003). Scientific triumphalism and learning from facts: Bacteriology and the 'Spanish flu' challenge of 1918. *Social History of Medicine, 16*(1), 97–110.

Trilla, A., Trilla, G., & Daer, C. (2008). The 1918 "Spanish flu" in Spain. *Clinical Infectious Diseases, 47*(5), 668–673.

Wu, W. Q. (2020). The historical data of pandemic influenza in China from 1918 to 1920 in the Shun Pao. *Zhonghua yi shi za zhi, 50*(4), 225–237.

CHAPTER 3

Unequal Mortality During the Spanish Flu

Abstract Determinants of pandemic-related mortality are not well understood. To begin with, there is no consensus on the best approach to count pandemic-related deaths. We argue that excess mortality is a good measure for the 1918 Flu in Spain, but it may not be suitable for other countries. There was substantial variation in excess mortality across occupations in Spain. The highest excess mortality was among low-income workers. In addition, there was a rural mortality penalty across all occupations that temporarily reversed the historical urban penalty. Climatic and economic conditions were correlated with excess mortality in the low-income groups but not in the middle and high-income ones. We conclude that the higher capacity of certain social groups to isolate themselves from social contact was behind these socioeconomic mortality differentials.

Keywords Health inequality · Socioeconomic mortality differences · Urban penalty

© The Author(s), under exclusive license to Springer Nature Switzerland AG 2022
S. Basco et al., *Pandemics, Economics and Inequality*,
Palgrave Studies in Economic History,
https://doi.org/10.1007/978-3-031-05668-0_3

Computing Mortality During Pandemics

Establishing the number of deaths and mortality rates during a pandemic is not a straightforward task.[1] For this reason, there are substantial contradictions in the number of deaths and mortality rates, among different sources. We have typically two contradictory sets of information on death rates: official figures computed by the health authorities with registrars' data and indirect estimates produced by independent researchers with the excess mortality method.

The independent estimates are more accurate than the official computations. The official estimates of pandemic mortality have a series of problems. First, figures are based on the questionable assumption that all cases are being tested and that tests are 100% accurate. Second, the mortality rates might be underestimated because of the time-lag bias associated with diagnosing and reporting cases. Therefore, the number of pandemic deaths at the beginning of the pandemic is likely to be underestimated. Third, once the pandemic advances, mortality might be overestimated due to the definition of what is a pandemic case.[2] For example, deaths of people with a positive test are directly associated with the pandemic even if they had mild illness symptoms and might have died due to another illness. Overall, the relevant literature has concluded that official figures underestimated pandemic deaths.

In the case of 1918 influenza, pharmacological flu tests were not available. Therefore, counting the number of cases was extremely difficult. During the period, health authorities produced statistics on the cause of death using observed symptoms. However, symptoms of flu-related deaths are akin to those of other pulmonary illnesses since influenza viruses can cause pneumonia. For this reason, official reports only recorded a portion of the overall flu-related deaths and grossly underestimated flu-related deaths.

To solve this underreporting issue, previous literature on the Spanish flu identifies all deaths associated with pulmonary illness in the official reports as flu-related.[3] However, this does not fully solve the underreporting problems. Some flu-related deaths are caused by a failure in other than non-respiratory organs and, hence, cannot be properly identified without pharmacological tests. Therefore, they were not classified as pulmonary-related deaths. As in recent pandemics, health authorities were likely underreporting flu-related mortality when the disease was rare and exaggerating its impact when it was widespread. Furthermore, without testing, the disparate behaviour of the different local doctors and registrars could also influence the reporting of the mortality causes. To complicate more the use of the official reports' evidence, flu and other pulmonary diseases mortality were common before 1918. Therefore, some mortality attributed to the 1918 influenza could be a consequence of other pulmonary illnesses or the regular flu strain.

Excess mortality provides an estimate of the additional number of deaths within a given period in a geographical region, compared to the number of expected deaths (Porta, 2014). The denominator of this calculation is computed using the same period in the preceding year or averaged over several preceding years. This method solves the reporting problems of the official statistics and offers a straightforward way for obtaining accurate mortality estimations.

The use of excess mortality method for computing deaths during the 1918 influenza is not without issues. The basic constraint of this method is that the baseline period should have a stable mortality pattern. With two, or more, successive mortality shocks, the excess mortality method results in misleading evidence. The baseline calculations are also erroneous when the structure of the population is incomplete in the years before the pandemic, and mortality rates typically differ by age group (Colvin & McLaughlin, 2021). This kind of reporting problem hampers estimations for all belligerent countries during World War I. For example, we cannot obtain an efficient baseline estimate of British mortality rates before the flu since a sizable portion of its population was fighting overseas.

Spain did not take part in World War I, and its population structure was complete. Therefore, this country offers a unique opportunity to study the real impact of the pandemic on mortality in all age groups. However, the Spanish official data on causes of death have the same underreporting problems. Spanish authorities have been producing death certificates since the nineteenth century. These documents contain a substantial amount of information on the deceased and the cause of death. The Spanish government also compiles national aggregate statistics (*Movimiento de la población de España*) employing direct information gathered by local registers. Previous studies on Spain have used this kind of data on the causes of death.[4] These studies associated all pulmonary deaths in 1918 with the flu pandemic. To minimize the double-counting of pulmonary deaths, they have deleted the expected number of deaths for these causes. However, all these computations are underreporting flu-related deaths because they do not avoid the registrars' bias in establishing mortality causes.

Alternatively, we use the excess mortality method according to the following equation[5]:

$$FED_i = 100 * \left[\frac{\text{Deaths in } 1918_i}{\text{Average Deaths Pre} - 1918_i} - 1\right] \quad (3.1)$$

where FED_i is flu excess deaths in group i. The Average Deaths Pre-1918 are computed using data between 1911 and 1917. Group i could be a month, a province, an occupation, people in each age/gender bin, or people in each occupation/sex. This mortality measure has many advantages: controls for previous mortality related to pulmonary illnesses, avoids the registrars' bias in determining the causes of death, accounts for seasonal mortality effects, and considers age differentials of mortality (even within socioeconomic groups and occupations).

A simple comparison of our new estimates with alternative measures shows how plausible this estimation is. In 1918, the Spanish registrars identified a total of 147,114 flu deaths and 117,778 deaths caused by other respiratory problems. In 1917, they recorded 7,749 flu deaths and 44,463 deaths caused by other respiratory problems. The total figure with our excess death method is 245,406. Note that this estimation seems highly plausible and lies between the registrar figures of flu and pulmonary-related deaths (264,892 deaths) and these figures minus the previous year's recorded deaths by seasonal flu and other respiratory illness (212,680 deaths).

UNEQUAL MORTALITY DURING THE SPANISH FLU

Modern pandemic mortality does not spread equally across human populations.[6] A large part of the variation in the pandemic mortality is unintended and difficult to avoid. Pandemic arrives earlier in some locations, and some ages (typically infants and elderly) have less self-protection against bacteria and viruses. Similarly, women, especially pregnant ones, are less protected against this type of disease. Genetic differences, and previous immunization to the pandemic, are sometimes behind sex and age mortality differentials (Noymer & Garenne, 2000). Some intrinsic characteristics of the affected locations like population density and climate can also account for these geographical diffusion patterns.[7]

However, one should also consider that some pandemic mortality differences are preventable since they are a consequence of failures in precautionary measures and health inequities. Government failures in informing and protecting the population explain a considerable amount of the geographic variation in mortality (Markel et al., 2007). Similarly, the absence of social capital exacerbates the consequences of pandemic shocks.[8] However, social group mortality differences are not easy to explain.[9] Living conditions can cause co-morbidity (poor housing, nutrition, and sanitation) and social-related illness. Poor people could not avoid social contact during pandemic outbursts and, hence, suffer a large proportion of infections. Finally, some jobs have a higher infection rate, and mortality risks, than others.

Sex and Age Differences

Morbidity and mortality are often higher for women than men during influenza outbreaks. Previous literature has related these differences to two causes: female pregnancy and genetic differences between sexes (Klein et al., 2012). Instead, COVID-19 produces more severe symptoms and higher mortality among men than among women.[10]

The common influenza age-specific mortality is "U-shaped". Therefore, high-mortality rates are among infants and the elderly, and low mortality in healthy persons between these ages.[11] In the case of Covid-19, age is a risk factor in rich-income countries but not in the middle- and low-income countries where age-related mortality curves are flat.[12]

The 1918 influenza had a unique age signature pattern.[13] Contrary to typical influenza, this pandemic had a relatively lower excess mortality for older adults, while excess mortality was higher from 20 to 40 years old. Previous research has argued that it was likely that older adults had already gone through other influenza episodes and had acquired immunity to the 1918 pandemic.

The pandemic in Spain followed this unique flu pattern. Figure 3.1. reports the excess death rates by age group and gender. Excess death rates follow an inverse U-shape: children and older adults had lower excess mortality rates than young people. The age group with the highest mortality rates was the age group from 25 to 34 years old. This age group had an excess death rate of above 200%. Older people (above 55 years old) had an excess death rate of below 40%. This figure also shows substantial differences between excess mortality in women and men. Overall, there was a female penalty: the total excess female mortality was 57% while the male one was 51%. Excess mortality for females was higher for those aged between 10 and 29. This evidence gives some support to the presumption that pregnancy accounted for a substantial part of higher female mortality.

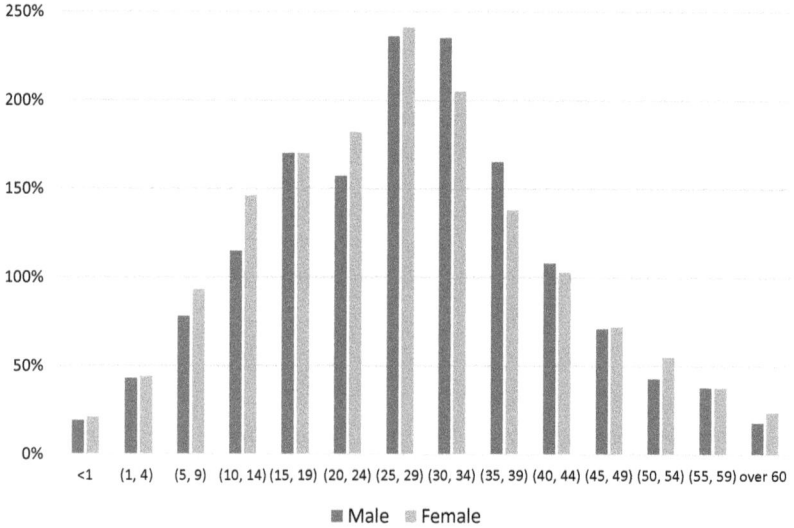

Fig. 3.1 Flu-related excess mortality by age and gender in Spain (*Notes* Excess mortality in 1918 computed using Eq. 3.1. We apply Eq. 3.1 for each sub-sample, so that, we compare, for example, deaths of females aged 20–24 in 1918 with the average deaths of females aged 20–24 before 1918. Original data as described in Chapter 3)

The Geographic Differences

Spanish provinces did not experience the pandemic with the same intensity. The following four maps present some basic information on the distribution of the pandemic (map at the high left corner) and some spatial correlates (atmospheric pressure, GDP per capita, and literacy).

The excess mortality followed a spatial pattern. The most affected provinces were in the North-West of Spain (North Castile and Leon). Other provinces affected by the highest mortality outside this epicentre of the pandemic were Biscay, Huelva, and Almeria. Interestingly, these three provinces were important mining locations. On a sharp contrast, Southern and Mediterranean provinces were among the least affected by the pandemic.

The spatial correlation between low pressure and Spain's pandemic intensity is apparent when one considers the climatic conditions during the Pandemic year (compare maps a and b). Map b reproduces the average atmospheric pressure during September and October of 1918 (Basco et al., 2021). Low pressure usually leads to cloudiness, wind, and precipitation but high pressure usually heads to fair, calm weather. This correlation between the climatic condition and contemporary influenza epidemics has been highlighted by a substantial literature.[14] Similarly, it has been alleged that the severity and timing of the 1918 influenza were correlated with rain and damp conditions.[15]

Some previous studies have concluded that socially disadvantaged locations were more affected by the pandemic mortality.[16] Typically, socioeconomic indicators considered are population density, illiteracy rates, homeownership rates, number of rooms per household, and unemployment.[17] Most of these studies show that the least developed regions tend to have higher mortality rates.

We map GDP per capita and literacy rates in the two bottom maps of Fig. 3.2. Clearly, the spatial correlation between GDPs per capita, literacy rates, and pandemic mortality is weak or non-existent. Some of the poorest Spanish provinces did not suffer higher pandemic mortality rates. In a similar vein, some of the provinces with the lowest literacy rates escaped the worst consequences of the 1918 influenza.

Socioeconomic Factors

There are contrasting views on the role of socioeconomic factors in determining influenza-related death rates during the 1918 pandemic. Research contemporary to the pandemic disagreed on the importance of socioeconomic factors in explaining mortality rates.[18] Recent literature, however, has pointed out the importance of socioeconomic indicators in accounting for pandemic mortality differentials (Mamelund et al., 2021). Grantz et al.'s (2016) studies on Chicago pointed out that social factors at the local level, such as literacy, homeownership, and unemployment, were associated with influenza and pneumonia mortality rates in 1918. Mamelund's (2006) study on two of Oslo's parishes found that those living in small apartments had the highest influenza-related death rate. The recent research of Bengtsson et al. (2018) using individual data on Sweden also found substantial class differences in excess mortality but no perfect class gradient. The skilled workers had a statistically significantly lower death rate than the low-skilled and unskilled workers during the pandemic period. However, the difference between the low-skilled and the unskilled was not statistically significant.

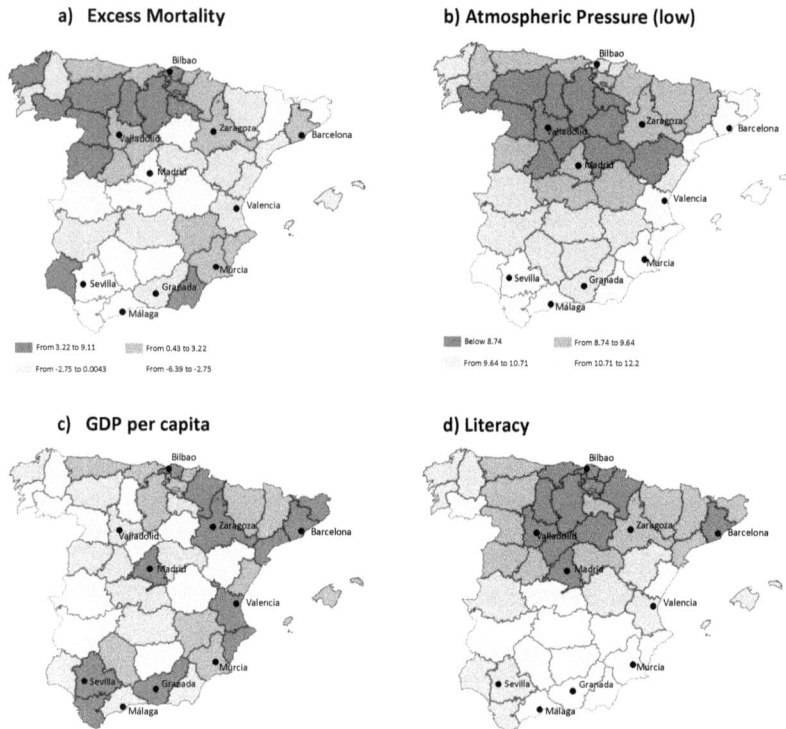

Fig. 3.2 Determinants of flu-related excess mortality in Spain (*Notes* All maps include the 10 largest capitals of provinces in 1910. Excess mortality is the province shift-share component of flu-related excess mortality [see Basco et al., 2021, for details]. For underlining mortality data see this chapter. Atmospheric pressure is a daily average during September and October of 1918. Data obtained from Goerlich Gisbert [2012]. Gross Domestic Product (GDP) per capita, in real terms, in 1910 from Rosés et al. [2010]. Literacy rates defined as share of people aged over 10 who could write and read. Data from Nuñez [1989])

Figure 3.3 reports the differences in excess mortality across different occupations separately by males and females (data from Basco et al., 2021). Children are in category xii (Unknown/Non-productive) and family carers (housewives) under category xi (No occupation). It is important to note that a relevant characteristic of Spanish labour markets in the 1910s was the substantial segregation by sex: men were rare in the

3 UNEQUAL MORTALITY DURING THE SPANISH FLU 41

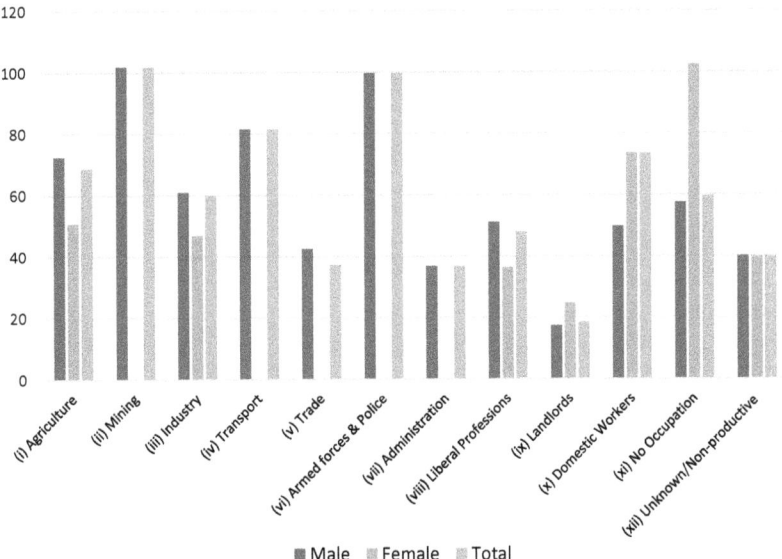

Fig. 3.3 Flu-related excess mortality across occupations in Spain (*Notes* See Fig. 3.1 and main text for the definition of excess mortality. We refer the reader to Basco et al. [2021] for more information about the method, sources and definition of occupations)

domestic sector while females were scarce, or absent, in mining, transport, trade, armed forces and police, and public administration. Furthermore, a well-known problem of the Spanish censuses is that many female agrarian workers were recorded under category xi (no occupation) or as domestic workers.[19] Thus, we should take the female excess mortality in agricultural occupations with a grain of salt.

Workers in mining, armed forces and police, and transportation (with increased death rates above 80%) experienced the highest increases in mortality. However, the highest excess mortality was recorded among females with no occupation with an astonishing 102%. The most abundant occupations in this period also suffered relatively higher excess mortality rates: agriculture (68%) and industry (about 60%). On the other side of the mortality spectrum, one can observe the lowest mortality rates among landlords (only 18%),[20] liberal professions (48%), administration (about 37%), and trade (37%).

We grouped the various occupations into three income groups: low, mid, and high. The low- and mid-income groups had similar excess mortality rates (69% and 62%, respectively), and the high-income group had the lowest recorded excess mortality (29%). In sum, this evidence indicates that socioeconomic factors were essential in explaining differences in mortality rates during the 1918 influenza.

The Rural Penalty in Flu Mortality

A substantial literature has documented the existence of an urban mortality penalty during industrialization processes. Mortality was higher among urban than rural inhabitants, after controlling for age and sex, in developed economies until, at least, World War II. This urban penalty disappeared due to substantial investments in urban sanitation and the diffusion of pharmaceutical measures against contagious illnesses.[21]

Spain also experienced this urban mortality penalty, at least, until the Spanish Civil War. However, the Spanish urban penalty was lower than in other European countries.[22] This lower penalty is likely due to the smaller size and slower industrialization of the Spanish cities that were, in consequence, less overcrowded. Martínez-Carrión and Moreno-Lázaro (2007) also document this urban penalty in the height of conscripts, particularly among those from a working-class background. This urban height penalty could indicate that the health condition of the urban populations was, on average, poorer than that of the rural ones.

During pandemics, the overcrowding and the poor living conditions in cities could result in more extensive contagion and thus higher mortality (Haines, 2001). However, living in cities can also provide some advantages in the prevention of pandemics. Urbanites may have better information on the evolution and dangers of influenza and might take more stringent social distance measures, thereby reducing contagion and mortality. Furthermore, income and wages were higher in Spanish cities than in the countryside[23] and, hence, urban workers could have more savings to keep the social distance and isolated at home.

Figure 3.4 reproduces the excess mortality differential between cities and rural locations for each occupation. The result of this exercise is self-evident: the rural mortality premium is higher across all different occupations. The extreme case is among trade workers for which rural mortality was 14 times higher than the urban one. Overall, excess rural mortality was about 58%, and urban one was about 52%; therefore, the rural penalty was more than 10%.

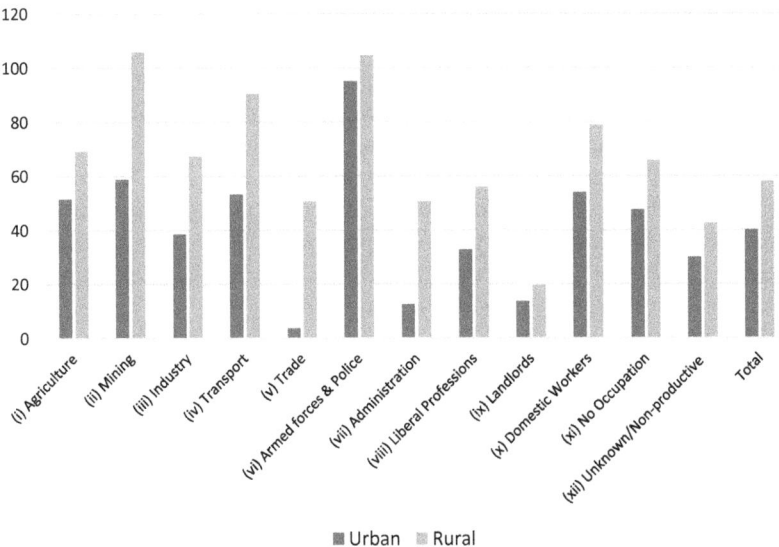

Fig. 3.4 Flu-related excess mortality in urban and rural locations in Spain (*Notes* See Basco et al. [2021] for more details on the definition of rural and urban)

Social Distancing and Mortality

Contagious pathogens can spread through social contact without pharmacological protective measures (Anderson & May, 1992). Consequently, people who meet many people are more susceptible to infectious disease transmission.[24] An obvious solution to this problem is the implementation of social distancing. Modern research has underlined that the success of this kind of measure depends not only on health authorities' strategies and resources but also on individual observance. External factors like information and local factors, such as infected family members or friends, determine individuals' disposition to observe social distancing.[25] However, social distance is not sometimes possible for lower-paid workers, particularly those engaged in certain essential activities or without personal economic means (Bambra et al., 2020).

The 1918 influenza had an extremely rapid development.[26] The incubation period was one to two days, and death could take quickly, within twelve to twenty-four hours of the first acute symptoms. Once the symptoms had developed, the mortality rate was staggering (60–70%). Morbidity rates were also very high. For example, from September through November 1918, the flu sickened 20 to 40% of US Army and Navy personnel. To sum up, the only way to stop the diffusion of the flu was the implementation of rapid curfews and social distancing.

Social distancing and curfews were not mandatory in Spain during the 1918 influenza. As we mentioned earlier, pandemic information was available and local and national newspapers published widely on its consequences. Therefore, it is likely that a large part of the population was aware of the deadliest results of the pandemic.

Our results are consistent with the view that flu contagion was higher in occupations where people were in close contact and moved across places. Mining workers had the additional disadvantage of working in locations with poor ventilation, where there was faster diffusion of the virus.[27] Similarly, people employed in the armed forces and police, and transportation had to move across places and, arguably, had high exposure to the flu. Also, the military personnel lived in barracks sleeping in communal dorms, which facilitated the spread of the flu. An interesting case is the workers in the trade sector. There were staggering differences in excess mortality between urban and rural workers. We can hypothesize that this is a consequence that urban trade took place in shops while the rural one was still itinerant with traders moving from one place to another.

Another plausible cause of the differences in mortality across occupations is the economic capacity of the individuals. Spain did not have public support for the unemployed during this period; so, individuals self-financed their absences from work and self-isolation measures. Therefore, workers in high-income occupations had the economic means (savings) to shield themselves from the pandemic. For example, it is plausible that landlords were more aware of the dangers of the flu, were not forced to leave the house to work, and kept social distancing due to their economic resources. A similar argument can explain the lower excess mortality of liberal professions and administration workers (public servants). A regression shows excess mortality among low-income workers is positively explained by climate (atmospheric pressure) and negatively by population density (a proxy for economic income). Instead, these two factors had no influence among excess mortality among mid- and high-income workers (Basco et al., 2021).

Finally, given that this urban mortality advantage was not due to structural health factors, it is likely that social distancing measures boosted by better information played a substantial role in these death differentials between cities and the countryside. Furthermore, these results also cast doubts about the hypothesis that previous sanitary or health conditions were decisive for differentials in pandemic-related mortality rates since health was poorer in the cities than in the countryside.

To conclude, we have seen that the Spanish Flu had a devastating mortality effect. In addition, flu-related mortality was unequal across occupations and regions, being, at least in Spain, relatively higher in lower-income workers and rural regions. In the next chapters, we will explain how this pandemic affected economic activity and the redistribution of resources within the economy.

Notes

1. Baud et al. (2020).
2. Beaney et al. (2020), and Spychalski et al. (2020).
3. See, for example, Chowell et al. (2008).
4. Echevarri (1985) and Chowell, Erkoreka, et al. (2014).
5. Basco et al. (2021) discuses more in detail the methodology.
6. Bambra et al. (2020), Chen and Krieger (2021), Feigenbaum et al. (2019) and Turner-Musa et al. (2020).
7. Mamelund (2011) and Clay et al. (2018, 2019).
8. Elgar et al. (2020) and Le Moglie et al. (2020).
9. Brown and Ravaillon (2020), Jay et al. (2020), and Mamelund (2017).
10. Takashahi et al. (2020).
11. Taubenberger et al. (2019).
12. See, Caramelo et al. (2020) on the evidence on the rich countries and Demombynes (2020) on the low and middle-income countries.
13. Luk et al. (2001), Schoenbaum (1996), and Simonsen et al. (2018).
14. Alonso et al. (2007), Bloom-Feshbach et al. (2013), and Tamerius et al. (2013).
15. Chowell, Erkoreka, et al. (2014), Chowell, Simonsen, et al. (2014) and Reyes et al. (2018).
16. Herring and Korol (2012), Mamelund (2006, 2018), Økland and Mamelund (2019), Sydenstricker (1931), Tuckel et al. (2006), Vaughan (1920), and Wilson et al. (2014).
17. Grantz et al. (2016), Mamelund (2006 , 2018), and Vaughn (1920).
18. See Bengtsson et al. (2018) for a review of the different views.
19. See, Gil Ibáñez (1978) and Nicolau (2005).

20. Basco et al. (2021) explain that this mortality difference across income groups cannot be explained by age-differences across occupations. Indeed, they use Population Census data to compute age-related excess mortality for each income group and show that the actual difference in excess mortality across groups is higher than the age-related one.
21. Cain and Hong (2009), Evans (2006), and Haines (2001).
22. Reher (2001), Ramiro and Sanz (1999), and García Gómez (2016).
23. See Rosés and Sánchez-Alonso (2004) on the evolution of the urban-rural wage gap during the period.
24. Nettle (2005) and Murray and Schaller (2016).
25. There is a growing literature on this issue. See, among others, Herrera-Diestra and Meyers (2019) and Kwok et al. (2020).
26. See, on these characteristics of the illness: Keeling (2020) and Byerly (2010).
27. Brundage and Shanks (2008).

References

Alonso, W. J., Viboud, C., Simonsen, L., Hirano, E. W., Daufenbach, L. Z., & Miller, M. A. (2007). Seasonality of influenza in Brazil: A traveling wave from the Amazon to the subtropics. *American Journal of Epidemiology, 165*(12), 1434–1442.

Anderson, R. M., & May, R. M. (1992). *Infectious diseases of humans: Dynamics and control* (28th ed.). Oxford University Press.

Bambra, C., Riordan, R., Ford, J., & Matthews, F. (2020). The COVID-19 pandemic and health inequalities. *Journal of Epidemiol Community Health, 74*(11), 964–968.

Basco, S., Domènech, J., & Rosés, J. R. (2021). *Unequal Mortality during the Spanish Flu* (CEPR Discussion Papers, 15783).

Baud, D., Qi, X., Nielsen-Saines, K., Musso, D., Pomar, L., & Favre, G. (2020). Real estimates of mortality following COVID-19 infection. *Lancet Infectious Diseases, 20*(7), 773.

Beaney, T., Clarke, J. C., Jain, V., Golestaneh, A. K., Lyons, G., Salman, D., & Majeed, A. (2020). Excess mortality: The gold standard in measuring the impact of COVID-19 worldwide? *Journal of the Royal Society of Medicine, 113*(9), 329–334.

Bengtsson, T., Dribe, M., & Eriksson, B. (2018). Social class and excess mortality in Sweden during the 1918 influenza pandemic. *American Journal of Epidemiology, 187*(12), 2568–2576.

Bloom-Feshbach, K., Alonso, W. J., Charu, V., Tamerius, J., Simonsen, L., Miller, M. A., & Viboud, C. (2013). Latitudinal variations in seasonal activity of influenza and respiratory syncytial virus (RSV): A global comparative review. *PLoS ONE, 8*(2), e54445.

Brown, C., & Ravallion, M. (2020). *Inequality and the coronavirus: Socioeconomic covariates of behavioral responses and viral outcomes across us counties* (NBER Working Papers, w27549).

Brundage, J. F., & Shanks, G. D. (2008). Deaths from bacterial pneumonia during 1918–19 influenza pandemic. *Emerging Infectious Diseases, 14*(8), 1193.

Byerly, C. R. (2010). The US military and the influenza pandemic of 1918–1919. *Public Health Reports, 125*(Supp. 3), 81–91.

Cain, L., & Hong, S. C. (2009). Survival in 19th century cities: The larger the city, the smaller your chances. *Explorations in Economic History, 46*(4), 450–463.

Caramelo, F., Ferreira, N., & Oliveiros, B. (2020). Estimation of risk factors for COVID-19 mortality-preliminary results. *MedRxiv*.

Chen, J. T., & Krieger, N. (2021). Revealing the unequal burden of COVID-19 by income, race/ethnicity, and household crowding: US county versus zip code analyses. *Journal of Public Health Management and Practice, 27*(1), S43–S56.

Chowell, G., Bettencourt, L. M., Johnson, N., Alonso, W. J., & Viboud, C. (2008). The 1918–1919 influenza pandemic in England and Wales: Spatial patterns in transmissibility and mortality impact. *Proceedings of the Royal Society B: Biological Sciences, 275*(1634), 501–509.

Chowell, G., Erkoreka, A., Viboud, C., & Echeverri-Dávila, B. (2014). Spatial-temporal excess mortality patterns of the 1918–1919 influenza pandemic in Spain. *BMC Infectious Diseases, 14*, 371.

Chowell, G., Simonsen, L., Flores, J., Miller, M. A., & Viboud, C. (2014). Death patterns during the 1918 influenza pandemic in Chile. *Emerging Infectious Diseases, 20*(11), 1803–1811.

Clay, K., Lewis, J., & Severnini, E. (2018). Pollution, infectious disease, and mortality: Evidence from the 1918 Spanish influenza pandemic. *Journal of Economic History, 78*(4), 1179–1209.

Clay, K., Lewis, J., & Severnini, E. (2019). What explains cross-city variation in mortality during the 1918 influenza pandemic? Evidence from 438 US cities. *Economics and Human Biology, 35*, 42–50.

Colvin, C. L., & McLaughlin, E. (2021). Death, demography and the denominator: Age-adjusted influenza-18 mortality in Ireland. *Economics and Human Biology, 41*, 100984.

Demombynes, G. (2020). *COVID-19 age-mortality curves are flatter in developing countries* (World Bank Policy Research Working Paper, 9313).

Echeverrri, B. (1985). *La gripe Española. La pandemia de 1918–1919*. Centro de Investigaciones Sociológicas (CIS).

Elgar, F. J., Stefaniak, A., & Wohl, M. J. (2020). The trouble with trust: Time-series analysis of social capital, income inequality, and COVID-19 deaths in 84 countries. *Social Science and Medicine, 263*, 113365.

Evans, R. (2006). *Death in Hamburg: Society and politics in the Cholera years 1830–1910*. Penguin.

Feigenbaum, J., Muller, C., & Wrigley-Field, E. (2019). Regional and racial inequality in infectious disease mortality in U.S. cities, 1900–1948. *Demography, 56*, 1371–1388.

García Gómez, J. J. (2016). Urban penalty en España: el caso de Alcoy (1857–1930). *Revista de Historia Industrial, 25*(63): 49–78.

Gil Ibáñez, S. (1978). Un intento de homogeneización de las clasificaciones profesionales en España (1860–1930). *Revista Internacional de Sociología, 25*, 7–40.

Goerlich Gisbert, F. J. (2012). Datos climáticos históricos para las regiones españolas. CRU TS 2.1. *Investigaciones de Historia Económica, 8*(1), 29–40.

Grantz, K. H., Rane, M. S., Salje, H., Glass, G. E., Schachterle, S. E., & Cummings, D. A. (2016). Disparities in influenza mortality and transmission related to sociodemographic factors within Chicago in the pandemic of 1918. *Proceedings of the National Academy of Sciences, 113*(48), 13839–13844.

Haines, M. R. (2001). The urban mortality transition in the United States, 1800–1940. *Annales de démographie historique, 1*, 33–64.

Herrera-Diestra, J. L., & Meyers, L. A. (2019). Local risk perception enhances epidemic control. *PLoS ONE, 14*(12), e0225576.

Herring, D. A., & Korol, E. (2012). The north-south divide: Social inequality and mortality from the 1918 influenza pandemic in Hamilton, Ontario. In M. Fahrni & E. W. Jones (Eds.), *Epidemic encounters: Influenza, society, and culture in Canada* (pp. 97–112). University of Toronto Press.

Jay, J., Bor, J., Nsoesie, E. O., Lipson, S. K., Jones, D. K., Galea, S., & Raifman, J. (2020). Neighbourhood income and physical distancing during the COVID-19 pandemic in the United States. *Nature Human Behaviour, 4*(12), 1294–1302.

Keeling, A. W. (2020). The 1918 influenza pandemic: Lessons from the past for a global community. *Health Emergency and Disaster Nursing, 7*(1), 27–28.

Klein, S. L., Hodgson, A., & Robinson, D. P. (2012). Mechanisms of sex disparities in influenza pathogenesis. *Journal of Leukocyte Biology, 92*(1), 67–73.

Kwok, K. O., Li, K. K., Chan, H. H. H., Yi, Y. Y., Tang, A., Wei, W. I., & Wong, S. Y. S. (2020). Community responses during early phase of COVID-19 epidemic, Hong Kong. *Emerging Infectious Diseases, 26*(7), 1575.

Le Moglie, M., Gandolfi, F., Alfani, G., & Aassve, A. (2020). *Epidemics and trust: The case of the Spanish Flu* (IGIER Working Papers, 661).

Luk, L., Gross, P., & Thompson, W. W. (2001). Observations on mortality during the 1918 influenza pandemic. *Clinical Infectious Diseases, 33*, 1375–1378.
Mamelund, S. E. (2006). A socially neutral disease? Individual social class, household wealth and mortality from Spanish influenza in two socially contrasting parishes in Kristiania 1918–19. *Social Science and Medicine, 62*(4), 923–940.
Mamelund, S. E. (2011). Geography may explain adult mortality from the 1918–20 influenza pandemic. *Epidemics, 3*, 46–60.
Mamelund, S. E. (2017). Social inequality—A forgotten factor in pandemic influenza preparedness. *Tidsskrift for Den norske legeforening*.
Mamelund, S. E. (2018). 1918 pandemic morbidity: The first wave hits the poor, the second wave hits the rich. *Influenza and Other Respiratory Viruses, 12*(3), 307–313.
Mamelund, S. E., Shelley-Egan, C., & Rogeberg, O. (2021). The association between socioeconomic status and pandemic influenza: Systematic review and meta-analysis. *PLoS ONE, 16*(9), e0244346.
Markel, H., Lipman, H. B., Navarro, J. A., Sloan, A., Michalsen, J. R., Stern, A. M., & Cetron, M. S. (2007). Nonpharmaceutical interventions implemented by US cities during the 1918–1919 influenza pandemic. *JAMA, 298*(6), 644–654.
Martínez-Carrión, J. M., & Moreno-Lázaro, J. (2007). Was there an urban height penalty in Spain, 1840–1913? *Economics and Human Biology, 5*, 144–164.
Murray, D. R., & Schaller, M. (2016). The behavioral immune system. *Advances in Experimental Social Psychology, 53*, 75–129.
Nettle, D. (2005). An evolutionary approach to the extraversion continuum. *Evolutionary Human Behavior, 26*, 363–373.
Nicolau, R. (2005). Población, salud y actividad. *Estadísticas históricas de España: siglo, XIX–XX*(I), 77–154.
Noymer, A., & Garenne, M. (2000). The 1918 influenza epidemic's effect on sex differentials in mortality in the United States. *Population and Development Review, 26*(3), 565–581.
Nuñez, C. E. (1989). *Alfabetización y crecimiento económico en la España contemporánea* (PhD thesis). University of Alcalá.
Økland, H., & Mamelund, S. E. (2019). Race and 1918 influenza pandemic in the United States: A review of the literature. *International Journal of Environmental Research and Public Health, 16*(14), 2487.
Porta, M. (Ed.). (2014). *A dictionary of epidemiology*. Oxford University Press.
Ramiro, D., & Sanz, A. (1999). Cambios estructurales en la mortalidad infantil y juvenil en España, 1860–1930. *Boletín de la ADE, 17*, 40–87.

Reher, D. S. (2001). In search of the 'urban penalty': Exploring urban and rural mortality patterns in Spain during the demographic transition. *International Journal of Population Geography, 7*, 105–127.

Rosés, J. R., Martínez-Galarraga, J., & Tirado, D. A. (2010). The upswing of regional income inequality in Spain (1860–1930). *Explorations in Economic History, 47*(2), 244–257.

Rosés, J. R., & Sánchez-Alonso, B. (2004). Regional wage convergence in Spain 1850–1930. *Explorations in Economic History, 41*(4), 404–425.

Schoenbaum, S. C. (1996). Impact of influenza in persons and populations. *Options for the Control of Influenza, III*, 17–25.

Simonsen, L., Chowell, G., Andreasen, V., Gaffey, R., Barry, J., Olson, D., & Viboud, C. (2018). A review of the 1918 herald pandemic wave: Importance for contemporary pandemic response strategies. *Annals of Epidemiology, 28*(5), 281–288.

Spychalski, P., Błażyńska-Spychalska, A., & Kobiela, J. (2020). Estimating case fatality rates of COVID-19. *Lancet Infectious Diseases, 20*(7), 774–775.

Sydenstricker, E. (1931). The incidence of influenza among persons of different economic status during the epidemic of 1918. *Public Health Reports (1896–1970)*, 154–170.

Takahashi, T., Ellingson, M. K., Wong, P., Israelow, B., Lucas, C., Klein, J., Silva, J., Mao, T., Oh, J. E., Tokuyama, M., & Lu, P. (2020). Sex differences in immune responses that underlie COVID-19 disease outcomes. *Nature, 588*(7837), 315–320.

Tamerius, J. D., Shaman, J., Alonso, W. J., Bloom-Feshbach, K., Uejio, C. K., Comrie, A., & Viboud, C. (2013). Environmental predictors of seasonal influenza epidemics across temperate and tropical climates. *PLOS Pathogens, 9*(3), e1003194.

Taubenberger, J. K., Kash, J. C., and Morens, D. M. (2019). The 1918 influenza pandemic: 100 years of questions answered and unanswered. *Science Translational Medicine, 11*(502).

Tuckel, P., Sassler, S., Maisel, R., & Leykam, A. (2006). The Diffusion of the influenza pandemic of 1918 in Hartford, Connecticut. *Social Science History, 30*(2), 167–196.

Turner-Musa, J., Ajayi, O., & Kemp, L. (2020, June). Examining social determinants of health, stigma, and COVID-19 disparities. *Healthcare, 8*(2), 168.

Vaughan, W. T. (1920). Influenza: An epidemiological study. *American Journal of Hygiene, iii*, 260

Wilson, N., Oliver, J., Rice, G., Summers, J. A., Baker, M. G., Waller, M., & Shanks, G. D. (2014). Age-specific mortality during the 1918–19 influenza pandemic and possible relationship to the 1889–92 influenza pandemic. *Journal of Infectious Diseases, 210*(6), 993–995.

CHAPTER 4

The Spanish Flu and the Labour Market

Abstract Which are the effects of pandemics on real wages? In a Malthusian (pre-industrial) economy, one would expect that population debacles increase real wages since resources (land) per head grew. However, in modern economies, pandemics may reduce consumption, which may affect labour demand and, thus, put downward pressure on real wages. During the Spanish Flu, Spanish real wages declined. The contraction was sharper in occupations in non-essential goods industries and in more urbanized provinces. This wage behaviour points out that demand factors drove the response of the labour market to the pandemic shock.

Keywords Malthusian economy · Inequality · Real wages · Labour demand

PANDEMICS AND WAGES: THE MALTHUSIAN VIEW

As we have described in previous chapters, income inequality is one of the most researched pandemic outcomes. In practice, as we will see, economists tend to consider income inequality through the lens of real wages. The Malthusian model is a common theoretical background for these empirical analyses.

© The Author(s), under exclusive license to Springer Nature
Switzerland AG 2022
S. Basco et al., *Pandemics, Economics and Inequality*,
Palgrave Studies in Economic History,
https://doi.org/10.1007/978-3-031-05668-0_4

A Malthusian (or pre-industrial) economy can be described by the following production function,

$$Y = AT^{\alpha}L^{1-\alpha}, \tag{4.1}$$

where A is total factor productivity, T is the stock of land and L is population. Note that this is a constant return to scale production function. In a Malthusian economy, land and labour are the main factors of production. Another assumption is that the level of technology, A, is constant over time.[1] In this Malthusian economy, firms are also price-takers and goods are homogenous. Real wages are determined by the marginal product of labour. Thus, it follows that,

$$\frac{W}{P} = (1-\alpha)A\left(\frac{T}{L}\right)^{\alpha} \tag{4.2}$$

Given that productivity, A, is constant and the stock of land, T, is fixed, a collapse in population size, L, and hence the amount of labour force, produces an increase in real wages. The reason is that this production function features decreasing marginal product of labour. Intuitively, given a fixed stock of land, the output increases at a decreasing rate for each additional worker.

Following an analogous argument, it is straightforward to compute real rents on land, which are equal to the marginal product of land.

$$\frac{R}{P} = \alpha A\left(\frac{L}{T}\right)^{1-\alpha} \tag{4.3}$$

A theoretical implication of this model is that the real return of land, R, increases with population, L. Furthermore, an increase in the amount of land, T, will generate more output but it will also expand overall labour demand. That is, labour and land are complementary. It readily follows that the ratio between wages, W, and land rents, R, is equal to,

$$\frac{W}{R} = \frac{1-\alpha}{\alpha}\frac{T}{L} \tag{4.4}$$

Thus, the ratio between wages and land rents (W/R) is inversely proportional to the ratio between land and labour (T/L). For this reason, W/R is a commonly used measure of income inequality, which falls when W/R increases (Alfani, 2021). In other words, in a Malthusian economy, pandemics (sharp reductions in population. L) are conducive to an increase in real wages and the subsequent reduction in income inequality.

Is the historical evidence on the Black Death consistent with the previous Malthusian hypothesis? The catastrophic mortality effects of the pandemic resulted in the complete disruption of production and markets. Jedwab et al. (2021) point out that real wages and GDP decreased during the first two years after the outburst of the pandemic. In the subsequent years, prices rocketed while nominal wages remained fixed, sometimes due to strict regulations. Therefore, in the initial phases, the Malthusian effect did not predominate.

What happened in the long run? A substantial literature has linked the Black Death with the European transition from a low-wage to a high-wage economy. The surviving workers were the great winners of this plague since their wages experienced substantial growth. However, some countries did not follow this pattern. For example, according to Álvarez-Nogal et al. (2021), Spanish real wages decreased because of the pandemic.

Does this inequality pattern in pandemics hold outside the Black Death episode? Scheidel's (2017) answer is an unambiguous yes. More recent work by Jordà et al. (2021), using cross-country long-run data and pandemics dating back to the fourteenth century, also agrees with Scheidel. So, these authors find that real wages growth, and the corresponding declining rents, could be associated with historical pandemics.

A more nuanced view emerges from a closer inspection of different historical episodes. In particular, this pattern is not observable in the seventeenth-century European plagues. They had substantial mortality: the deadliest plagues were in Naples (1656–1658) with 15 million (normalized) deaths, Spain (1592–1602) with 9 million deaths, and in Italy (1629–1631) with 4 million deaths.[2] Despite the dramatic mortality, the Malthusian mechanism did not work since neither an increase in real wages nor a decrease in inequality were observable in these countries.[3]

There is no broad consensus on why equality gains did not follow catastrophic mortality.[4] For example, labour productivity may have decreased because of the plague. In Eq. 4.2, if A (productivity) decreases, it puts downward pressure on real wages, which may offset the direct effect of having a lower population, L. Others have argued that the existence of institutional arrangements limited nominal wage growth: therefore, labour productivity gains did not lead to wage increases.

The Spanish Flu and Real Wages

We now turn to the Spanish Flu. Even though there was some heterogeneity in the timing of the Spanish Flu across countries (see Chapter 2), the most common pattern is that the excess flu mortality started in 1918 and finished by 1920. It was a worldwide pandemic, with an estimated average death toll of 58.5 million, which would be equivalent to 193 million deaths today (Cirillo & Taleb, 2020).[5] Thus, even though the death rate was significantly lower than during the Black Death, it was well above that of, for example, the sixteenth-century plagues. Indeed, as Table 1.1 in Chapter 1 illustrated, the Spanish Flu belongs, at least, in the top-4 of deadliest pandemics of history. Did the Spanish Flu pandemic affect real wages like the Black Death?

Before turning to the data, it is essential to review the characteristics of the world economy when the Spanish Flu arrived. Most of the early twentieth century developed countries had expanded their economies beyond the limits of the Malthusian trap.[6] In other words, the development of population and welfare had escaped from the resource constraints. Interestingly, several developed countries had completed the demographic transition and were in a phase of relatively low mortality and birth rates.[7] Despite the Great War disruption, the resources constraints had not returned, and Malthusian positive checks were absent in almost all developed economies. The situation was not so favourable in the less developed countries. During the first decades of the twentieth century, many of these countries had not already escaped the resources constraint and, from time to time, experienced dramatic famines. Therefore, they were still in the Malthusian trap. In any case, it seems clear that the world economy was more developed than during the Black Death when the Malthusian constraint was binding and famines were ubiquitous.

Spain was a relatively backward country but was closer to the developed economies than to the underdeveloped ones.[8] The Malthusian positive check was not present, and the country was in the middle of the demographic transition.[9] However, the country was very unequal and heterogeneous.[10] Some regions were mainly industrial and urban and were practically finishing the demographic transition. In these modern regions, mortality and birth rates were relatively low and similar to those prevalent in the richest European countries. In contrast, other parts of the country were rural, agrarian, and had a more traditional demographic system. This spatial heterogeneity will allow us to compare more traditional and underdeveloped regions with more modern ones within the same country.

An important caveat when examining the effects of the Spanish Flu on real wages is that the spurt of the pandemic overlapped with the last months of the Great War. The Great War finished on the 11th of November 1918 when Germany signed the armistice. As we explained in Chapter 2, many countries experienced the first mild pandemic wave in the Spring of 1918. Furthermore, the pandemic peak was in October or November.

The Great War may widely affect the estimation of the effects of the pandemic on real wages in multiple ways. First, as we also explained in Chapter 3, measures of excess mortality cannot be applied because war-related deaths are impossible to distinguish from flu-related ones.[11] Second, the absence of information on the pandemic due to military censorship could also distort the response of the economic agents. Third, governments' interventions due to the war distorted the belligerents' economies.[12] In particular, price and wage controls altered the free operation of labour markets. Simultaneously, unemployment practically disappeared due to mass mobilization and massive public investments in the war effort. Finally, the end of the war further altered the unfettered operation of the labour markets. In all belligerent countries, the massive demobilization, and the reorganization of the production towards a peaceful economy resulted in high unemployment and a dramatic economic crisis. The situation was even worst among the countries that lost the Great War since political and social conflicts were ubiquitous.[13]

In sharp contrast with the belligerent countries, Spain is a more suitable laboratory to study the impact of the pandemic on real wages. First, since Spain did not suffer war-related deaths, pandemic mortality data are more exact. Second, news of the pandemic circulated widely and rapidly; so, economic agents could react to them. Third, the Spanish government did not intervene in factor markets and there were no massive public investments for war preparation. However, the Great War had some influence on the Spanish economy.[14] The country experienced substantial inflation and an export boom. The end of the war also led to an overproduction crisis when the economies of the belligerent countries resumed their normal production patterns.

Before considering the effect of pandemics, let us briefly describe a simple labour market equilibrium. As in any market, labour supply and demand determine the equilibrium wage. For simplicity, we assume that there are no minimum wages or other institutional rigidities. We postulate that labour supply is elastic. It implies that an increase in the nominal wage raises the price of leisure and, thus, encourages households to work more hours. Profit maximizing firms choose labour demand. Since the wages are the price of workers, labour demand will decrease with wages. Given wages, a firm will want to hire more workers, for example, when the product demand increases. The firm may also want to hire more workers when labour productivity grows.

Which are the effects of pandemics on labour markets? Theoretically, pandemics may affect the labour market through labour supply and demand. First, the labour supply declines because there are fewer workers available. Several different situations can generate these labour supply reductions. Workers can die and cannot be replaced immediately by new workers. They can also get infected and become sick, not attending their jobs. Or they become scared of going to work and are, thus, less willing to work. Second, the pandemic reduces goods demand. Subsequently, firms reduce labour demand. As with labour supply, the labour demand constraint could have different causes. High mortality reduces overall consumption. People may fear losing their job and increase savings reducing consumption. Lockdowns or other government regulations may force firms to restrict sales. In addition, people scared of getting infected may reduce non-essential (luxury) goods demand.

Figure 4.1 illustrates these two channels and considers two possible outcomes. Point 0 represents the pre-pandemic equilibrium. The supply effect represents a shift of the labour supply curve (L^S) to the left. If this is the only effect, point 1 in Fig. 4.1 is the new equilibrium. In this situation, real wages are higher than before the pandemic. Intuitively, the reason is that firms have not changed labour demand, but there are fewer workers available, which increases wages. According to the evidence reported before, point 1 would be the most common outcome during the Black Death. However, this initial result may change once we include the demand effect. The demand effect is a leftward shift in the demand curve, which puts downward pressure on real wages. Point 2 in Fig. 4.1 represents a case in which the demand effect dominates and real wages are below pre-pandemic levels. The reason is that the decline in firms' demand offsets reductions in labour supply. In principle, it is ambiguous which effect should dominate. Therefore, the pandemic effect on real

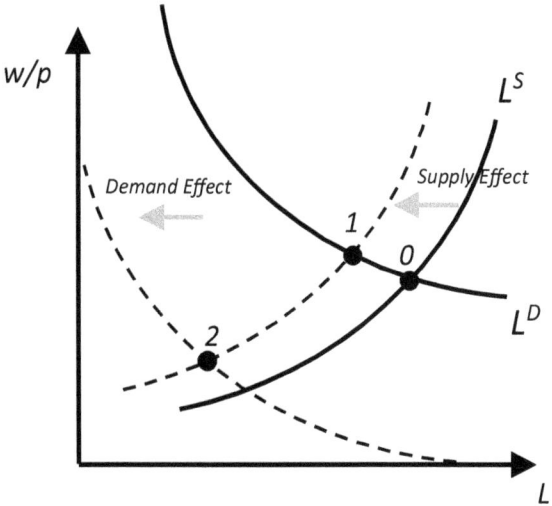

Fig. 4.1 Theoretical effect of pandemics on real wages (*Notes* Graphical summary of the effects of pandemics on real wages. L^S and L^D stand for labor supply and labor demand, respectively. Dots represent the equilibrium in the labor market for the three different assumptions made in the text)

wages will depend on the relative demand and supply effects, which, in principle, may differ across occupations and regions.

We are now ready to document the effect of the Spanish Flu on real wages. There is relatively little evidence on this issue, partly due to its interaction with the Great War. For the United States, Garret (2009) reports that, at the state level, there was a positive correlation between influenza mortality per capita (1918–1919) and real manufacturing wage growth (1914–1919). Therefore, at least for this country, the supply effect offset the demand one. The pandemic mortality consequences for the Swedish labour market were different. Karlsson et al. (2014) documents that flu-related mortality did not impact nominal earnings (which included pensions) but increased poorhouse rates. Thus, for Sweden, a country with moderate mortality rates (5.9 per 1000),[15] one can suppose that labour demand contraction counterbalanced pandemic mortality (labour supply). For Italy, Galletta and Giommoni (2020) argue, using municipality-level data, that income inequality measured with the Gini coefficient increased due to the Spanish Flu. Therefore, the Italian experience is closer to the Swedish than the US one.[16]

We will devote the remaining part of this chapter to the Spanish case from which we hand-collected data and carefully identified its effects (Basco et al., 2021). Apart from the reasons mentioned above, there are, at least, two other reasons that make Spain an excellent case study. Spain's death rates were one of the highest in Europe (see Table 1.2 in Chapter 1). Therefore, if supply-side factors predominated, they should be apparent in the Spanish data. Furthermore, the country had excellent data on mortality, wages, and consumer prices, which allows us to conduct this detailed analysis.[17] We also want to remind the reader that, as explained in Chapter 2, the pandemic mortality happened in 1918. Thus, it is plausible that the effects on the labour market were apparent in that year. To empirically identify the effect of the Spanish Flu on real wages, we employ the following standard differences-in-differences specification:

$$\Delta Y_{ct} = \beta_t \sum_{t=t_c}^{T} \text{Flu}_c \cdot D_t + \gamma Y_{ct-1} + \delta_c + \delta_t + \varepsilon_{ct}, \qquad (4.5)$$

where ΔY_{ct} is annual growth rate of real wages, Y_{ct} is (log) real wage in province c in year t, Flu_c is excess mortality during the Spanish Flu (year 1918) in province c (as a measure of flu-related mortality), and δ_c and δ_t are province and year fixed effects. D_t is a dummy equal to one for period t and 0 otherwise. The period of this analysis is 1915–1930. For ease of exposition, we focus on the following specification. $D_{1918} = 1$ for year 1918 and $D_{\text{Post-1918}} = 1$ for all years after 1918. This specification allows us to separately identify the short-run and the potential long-run effect. Basco et al. (2021) also consider a specification with the overall flu effect by including only $D_{\text{Post-1917}} = 1$ for years after 1917 and 0 otherwise. Note that β inform us on whether provinces with more excess mortality during the Spanish Flu had higher wage growth during (after) the Spanish Flu than before.[18]

Table 4.1 reproduces the results on the effects on real wages for different occupations. We consider 9 occupations, (i) agricultural workers, (ii) builders, (iii) stone cutters, (iv) carpenters, (v) blacksmiths, (vi) metal workers, (vii) painters, (viii) tailors, and (ix) shoemakers. The use of real wage data for different occupations is important because labour supply and demand shifts could have differed across industries. For example, if the demand shock predominated over the supply shock, real wages in

Table 4.1 Effect of the Spanish Flu on real wages in Spain, by occupation

	(1) Agriculture	(2) Builder	(3) Stone Cutter	(4) Carpenter	(5) Blacksmith	(6) Metal	(7) Painter	(8) Tailor	(9) Shoemaker
Flu $1918_c * D_{1918}$	−19.23***	−10.10***	−8.13***	−7.07***	−6.02***	−1.54	−5.99	−15.84***	−23.45***
	(2.83)	(2.68)	(2.22)	(2.10)	(1.69)	(2.33)	(6.07)	(1.76)	(0.70)
Flu $1918_c * D_{\text{Post-1918}}$	−4.16	−6.51*	−9.25***	−6.32**	−3.38	−3.51	−0.95	−3.67	−2.44*
	(3.12)	(3.23)	(2.97)	(2.84)	(2.53)	(2.58)	(6.20)	(2.39)	(1.30)
Lag Real Wage$_{ct}$	−0.61***	−0.56***	−0.52***	−0.51***	−0.52***	−0.45***	−0.44***	−0.44***	−0.52***
	(0.08)	(0.07)	(0.06)	(0.07)	(0.08)	(0.06)	(0.07)	(0.06)	(0.09)
Province FE	Y	Y	Y	Y	Y	Y	Y	Y	Y
Year FE	Y	Y	Y	Y	Y	Y	Y	Y	Y
Observations	720	720	720	720	720	720	720	720	720

Notes The dependent variable is the annual growth rate of real wage for province and year. Flu 1918 is the value of excess mortality in 1918. D_{1918} is a dummy equal to one for year 1918. D_t is a dummy equal to one for year (period) t and zero otherwise. $t = $ Pre-1918 is omitted from the regressions and it is the control period. The table reports fixed effects regressions weighted by population. Standard errors in brackets are clustered at the year level. *$p < 0.10$, **$p < 0.05$, ***$p < 0.01$. The data is drawn from Basco et al. (2021)

non-essential consumption industries (like tailors or shoemakers) should decrease more than those in the essential sectors (like agriculture or construction).

The short-run flu effect, β_{1918}, is negative and statistically significant for all occupations (except for metal workers and painters). Note that there is substantial variation in this flu effect across industries. Indeed, real wages did not significantly change for some jobs, whereas these estimates imply that, for example, for shoemakers, they fell, on average, around 30%. Thus, at least for Spain, we can conclude that the short-run effect on real wages was negative and generalized throughout the economy. In addition, we find that it was stronger for tailors and shoemakers, which suggests that the demand effect played a decisive role in shaping the response of the Spanish labour market to the Spanish Flu. However, this negative effect was mostly short-lived. The estimates for the long-run effect, $\beta_{\text{Post-1918}}$, are negative, but they are not statistically significant for most occupations. This conclusion is confirmed in Basco et al. (2021) when they look at the overall flu effect (i.e., post-1917).

Spain was a very heterogenous country at the start of the twentieth century. Chapter 3 shows that excess mortality rates differed substantially in the various provinces. The most urbanized and industrialized provinces had lower death rates than many agrarian ones. Industrialization and urbanization were related but not perfectly correlated. For example, Madrid was a very urbanized but poorly industrialized province, whereas Girona (Catalonia) was a very industrialized province with a low urbanization rate.

Theoretically, these differences in urbanization and industrialization should help us to shed light on the relative importance of the demand and supply channels. According to a supply-driven interpretation, real wage reductions should be less intense in more industrialized provinces since worker shortages should be more relevant for labour-intensive sectors like manufacturing.

Regarding urbanization, as explained in Chapter 3, one distinctive feature of the geographical heterogeneity of excess mortality during the Spanish Flu in Spain is that there was an urban premium. That is, denser (more urbanized) regions had lower mortality. A plausible explanation is that urbanites took more precautions on the pandemics and tended to self-isolate more. There are likely causes for this differential urban behaviour: they were more informed about the pandemic (through newspapers, which circulated abundantly in cities), and they enjoyed higher incomes, which could allow them not to go to work. According to a demand-driven interpretation, this kind of behaviour implies that the negative effect of the pandemic in real wages could be exacerbated in more urbanized (denser) provinces because their populations reduced relatively more non-essential consumption.

Basco et al. (2021) formally test the previous hypotheses and their findings lend support to the demand-driven interpretation. Indeed, their regressions show that the negative effects of excess mortality on real wages were exacerbated in more urbanized regions, while the effects were not attenuated in more industrialized provinces. Thus, the overall evidence suggests that during the Spanish Flu, at least in Spain, the reduction of labour demand dominated over the contraction of labour supply and real wages fell.

To summarize, according to the evidence collected in Chapters 3 and 4, the Spanish flu was not a levelling event, at least, in Spain. Quite the contrary, among the less affluent members of the Spanish society, pandemic mortality was the highest, and real wages decreased due to the 1918 flu since the demand forces outweighed the supply ones.

Notes

1. Alfani (2021) offers a succinct justification of these assumptions for the pre-industrial economy. A vast economic literature has been devoted to understanding the evolution of technology, A, over time but this is outside the scope of this book. We refer the reader to specialized monographs like Galor (2011) or Acemoglu and Robinson (2013).
2. This data on mortality is from Cirillo and Taleb (2020).
3. For example, Alfani (2021) reproduces the evolution of real wages for Milan and Valencia during their respective plagues and it is apparent that real wages did not increase after the plague.
4. Alfani (2021) describes some arguments to explain this violation.
5. This is a conservative estimate since there are other estimates with higher mortality. According to Johnson and Mueller (2002), the death toll could be as high as 100 million people.
6. See, for example, Clark (2008) and Deaton (2013).
7. There is an ample literature on the demographic transition. See, among others, Lee (2003), Galor (2011), and Reher (2011).
8. See, for example, Prados de la Escosura (2017) and Prados de la Escosura and Sánchez-Alonso (2020).
9. See, among others, Arango (1980) and Pérez Moreda at al. (2015).

10. The period also witnessed the peak on regional inequality. On Spanish regional differences, see, for example, Rosés et al. (2010) and Martínez-Galarraga et al. (2015).
11. A related problem is that much of the flu excess mortality was concentrated among young adults, who were not living in the country and were fighting in different war fronts. In other words, many of the flu-related deaths could have been registered as war-related death since they happened among soldiers who became ill.
12. On the economic impact of the Great War, see the volumes of Broadberry and Harrison (2005, 2018).
13. Finally, even though it is not a major concern for the countries highlighted in the book, the Spanish Flu also coincided with the Treaty of Versailles (1919). As forecasted by Keynes (1920), this treaty had short and medium-run effects in Germany, which adds difficulty to disentangle the effects of the pandemic. Johnson and Mueller (2002) reports that the death rate of Spanish Flu was 3.8 per 1000 people in Germany (comparable to England, 5.8, but substantially below Italy, 10.7, or Spain, 12.3).
14. On the consequences of the Great War in Spain, see the classical study of García Delgado et al. (1973) and the recent one of Sudrià (2021).
15. These data are from Johnson and Mueller (2002).
16. A shortcoming of this paper is that they can only compute the Gini coefficient for 1918 and 1924, thereby missing short-run effects.
17. Basco et al. (2021) describe the data on real wages along with their original sources.
18. We refer the reader to Basco et al. (2021) for a careful discussion of this specification, assumption, and robustness to alternative specifications.

References

Acemoglu, D., & Robinson, J. (2013). *Why national fail: The origins of power, prosperity, and poverty.* Crown Business.

Alfani, G. (2021). Epidemics, inequality and poverty in preindustrial and early industrial times. *Journal of Economic Literature*, forthcoming.

Álvarez Nogal, C., Prados de la Escosura, L., & Santiago Caballero, C. (2021). *Economic effects of the Black Death: Spain in European perspective* (Instituto Figuerola Working Papers in Economic History, 2020-06).

Arango, J. (1980). La teoría de la transición demográfica y la experiencia histórica. *Reis, 10*(1), 169–198.

Basco, S., Domènech, J., & Rosés, J. R. (2021). The redistributive effects of pandemics: Evidence from the Spanish flu. *World Development, 141*, 105389.

Broadberry, S. N., & Harrison, M. (Eds.). (2005). *The economics of World War I*. Cambridge University Press.
Broadberry, S., & Harrison, M. (Eds.). (2018). *The economics of the Great War: A centennial perspective*. CEPR Press.
Cirillo, P., & Taleb, N. N. (2020). Tail risk of contagious diseases. *Nature Physics, 16*, 606–613.
Clark, G. (2008). *A farewell to Alms*. Princeton University Press.
Deaton, A. (2013). *The great escape*. Princeton University Press.
Galletta, S., & Giommoni, T. (2020). The effect of the 1918 influenza pandemic on income inequality: Evidence from Italy (COVID Economics: Vetted and Real-time Papers 33).
Galor, O. (2011). *Unified growth theory*. Princeton University Press.
García Delgado, J. L., Roldán, S., & Muñoz, J. (1973). *La Formación de la Sociedad Capitalista en España (1914–1920)*. CECA.
Garrett, T. A. (2009). War and pestilence as labor market shocks: US manufacturing wage growth 1914–1919. *Economic Inquiry, 47*(4), 711–725.
Jedwab, R., Johnson, N., & Koyama, M. (2021). The economic impact of the Black Death. *Journal of Economic Literature*, forthcoming.
Johnson, N., & Mueller, J. (2002). Updating the accounts: Global mortality of the 1918–1920 "Spanish" influenza pandemic. *Bulletin of the History of Medicine, 76*, 105–115.
Jordà, Ò., Singh, S. R., & Taylor, A. M. (2021). Longer-run economic consequences of pandemics. *Review of Economics and Statistics*, forthcoming.
Karlsson, M., Nilsson, T., & Pichler, S. (2014). The impact of the 1918 Spanish flu epidemic on economic performance in Sweden: An investigation into the consequences of an extraordinary mortality shock. *Journal of Health Economics, 36*(1), 1–19.
Keynes, J. M. (1920). *The economic consequences of peace*. Macmillan.
Lee, R. (2003). The demographic transition: Three centuries of fundamental change. *Journal of Economic Perspectives, 17*(4), 167–190.
Martínez-Galarraga, J., Rosés, J. R., & Tirado, D. A. (2015). The long-term patterns of regional income inequality in Spain, 1860–2000. *Regional Studies, 49*(4), 502–517.
Pérez Moreda, V., Reher, D. S., & Gimeno, A. S. (2015). La conquista de la salud: Mortalidad y modernización en la España contemporánea. *Madrid, 75*, 87–110.
Prados de la Escosura, L. (2017). *Spanish economic growth, 1850–2015*. Palgrave Macmillan.
Prados de la Escosura, L. P., & Sánchez-Alonso, B. (2020). Economic development in Spain, 1815–2017. In *Oxford Research Encyclopedia of Economics and Finance*. Oxford University Press.

Reher, D. S. (2011). Economic and social implications of the demographic transition. *Population and Development Review, 37*(1), 11–33.

Rosés, J. R., Martínez-Galarraga, J., & Tirado, D. A. (2010). The upswing of regional income inequality in Spain (1860–1930). *Explorations in Economic History, 47*(2), 244–257.

Scheidel, W. (2017). *The great leveler: Violence and the history of inequality from the stone age to the twenty-first century*. Princeton University Press.

Sudrià, C. (2021). A hidden fight behind neutrality. Spain's struggle on exchange rates and gold during the Great War. *European Review of Economic History, 25*(3), 549–570.

CHAPTER 5

The Spanish Flu and the Capital Market

Abstract In this section, we discuss how pandemics affect the returns to capital. First, we explain how pre-industrial pandemics distorted capital (land) returns and review the existing empirical literature. Then, we focus on modern pandemics and explain their effect on housing. For modern pandemics, we focus on housing since it is the most important physical asset in industrialized economies. Lastly, we review the consequences of the Spanish Flu in Spanish housing markets and argue that modern pandemics may change capital allocation across regions.

Keywords Land · Capital · Credit · Housing · Urban · Rural · Pandemics · Structural change

PANDEMICS AND CAPITAL RETURNS

In Chapter 4, we have considered the consequences of pandemics on the labour market. For most of the population, the evolution of real wages is the main determinant of households' income and consumption. However, capital returns (the other component of aggregate income) are equally important in determining income inequality and it is sometimes a factor behind social conflict. For this reason, we will devote this chapter to understand the effect of pandemics on capital returns.

The first difficulty to consider when analysing the evolution of capital returns lies in the definition of capital. There is not a clear-cut definition of capital. However, we will think of capital as "assets". The Merrian-Webster dictionary defines assets as: "something that it is owned by a person company, etc.". Examples of assets include machines, stocks, houses, or land.[1] As the reader can readily notice, the relative importance of each asset has changed over time. In a Malthusian (pre-industrial) world, the main asset in the economy was land. However, in the industrialized world, housing has become the largest and most important asset class (Jordà et al., 2019).[2] Thus, we will be interested in the effect of pandemics on land for the pre-industrialized period, and we will focus on housing for modern pandemics.

There are many reasons why the focus on housing prices is particularly informative. As the Great Recession has demonstrated, changes in real estate prices affect aggregate consumption, borrowing, investment, and even total factor productivity.[3] Furthermore, in the early twentieth century, the quality and affordability of the dwellings had a strong influence on population health and life expectancy.

Pre-industrial Pandemics and Land Rents

We divide this section into two parts. First, we develop a theoretical framework to explain the determinants of land returns (rents) in the Malthusian economy and how pandemics may affect them. Second, we review the empirical evidence on land returns' evolution after pre-industrialized world pandemics.

As explained in previous Chapter 4, a Malthusian (pre-industrial) economy can be described by the following production function,

$$Y = F(A, T, L) = AT^{\alpha}L^{1-\alpha}, \tag{5.1}$$

where A is total factor productivity, T is the stock of land, and L is population. In addition, it is assumed that the level of technology is constant.

Readers who are familiar with modern introductory macroeconomic textbooks will realize that Eq. (5.1) is the standard Cobb–Douglas production function where land (T) replaces capital (K). As we have argued, the most important asset in a Malthusian economy was land. The Cobb–Douglas production function has been widely used in economics, but we need to discuss its properties because the results will hinge on them.

One first property is that aggregate production increases with the stock of land (i.e., $F_T \equiv \frac{\partial F(.)}{\partial T} > 0$). This assumption seems appropriate for a Malthusian economy. If we think of an agricultural society, given the number of farmers (population), if they have more land available, they will produce more output.

A second, and crucial, property is that the marginal productivity of land increases with the number of farmers (population). Mathematically, it implies that $F_{TL} \equiv \frac{\partial^2 F(.)}{\partial T \partial L} > 0$. Intuitively, it means that, given the size of land, if more farmers work this land, they generate more output per land unit. In pre-industrial Europe, there were several ways to get these output increases. For example, output per land unit could increase with more intensive cultivation, replacing husbandry with farming, or cultivating new products like the potato. These positive effects have some limits (congestion). For each additional farmer, the extra output could diminish; in other words, it is subject to decreasing returns. However, we assume that the economy is not in a situation in which additional farmers have zero effect on extra output.

We follow the previous literature and consider the Cobb–Douglas production function. One particularity of the Cobb–Douglas production function is that the elasticity of substitution between land and farmers (workers) is one.[4] Real land rents are determined, in this economy, by the marginal product of land. According to Eq. (5.1), they are given by the next expression,

$$\frac{R}{P} = \alpha A \left(\frac{L}{T}\right)^{1-\alpha} \quad (5.2)$$

How did pandemics affect land rents? We assume that the stock of land employed in production remained intact, and the number of workers fell during pandemics. This assumption implies that land per farmer (T/L) increased. From Eq. 5.2, an increase in land per worker (T/L) reduces land rents. Remember that α is the land income share, a constant number between 0 and 1. Thus, if we assume that pandemics only affect the population (not the amount of land in use), taking the derivative of Eq. (5.2) with respect to L, we obtain the effect of increased mortality.

$$\frac{\partial R/P}{\partial L} = \alpha(1-\alpha)A\left(\frac{T}{L}\right)^{\alpha} T > 0 \qquad (5.3)$$

Equation 5.3 formally shows that pandemics (a drop in the number of farmers) will reduce the returns to land. The reason is that the marginal product of land decreases with fewer farmers working in each land unit. By looking at Eq. 5.3, we also observe that the size of the effect will depend on country endowments (that is, population/farmers per unit of land). When the land endowment is higher (α close to one) or lower (α close to zero), pandemic shocks would not affect the returns to land. Indeed, according to Eq. 5.3, the negative effects of pandemics on the real return to land are maximized when $\alpha = 1/2$.

After deriving the theoretical prediction on the effects of pandemics on land returns, let us discuss the relevant empirical literature. Unfortunately, there is scarce direct evidence on land prices. As we described in Chapter 4, there is a growing literature analysing the effects of pandemics on inequality. For example, Alfani (2022) explains that the Black Death led to an income inequality reduction in most countries. However, Alfani's arguments are predominantly based on the behaviour of real wages.[5]

As indirect evidence to analyse the effect of pandemics on land, we can refer to the literature on wealth inequality. The distribution of physical assets across the population determines wealth inequality. Note that changes in wealth distribution are not only caused by changes in the return of the assets of the wealthy. In other words, wealth inequality may decline for two reasons. First, there is a redistribution of assets from affluent towards less affluent people. Second, there is the price effect, that is, the relative return on assets owned by the wealthy declines.

Alfani (2015) uses property taxes in Piedmont to analyse the evolution of wealth inequality between the thirteenth and eighteenth centuries. He shows that the Black Death was conducive to a decline in wealth inequality. This finding is consistent with other case studies for the Black Death.[6] However, we do not know the causes of this decrease in inequality because both the price effect and the redistribution of assets could lead to changes in the wealth distribution. Given the mortality shock that the Black Death represented, it is likely that the second effect was especially relevant, and some wealthy households were unable to keep their properties when their land rents collapsed. In this sense, Alfani (2022) explains how Italian institutions changed after the Black Death to guarantee that wealthy people would keep control of their possessions in future pandemics. He argues that higher protection of the assets owned by wealthy Italians could explain why seventeenth-century pandemics in Italy were not conducive to a fall in wealth inequality.

Jordà et al. (2021) consider a cross-section of countries and explore the effect of pandemics on the return of real assets. Their dataset goes back to the fourteenth century. Therefore, it includes the Black Death. A major concern with this exercise is that it mixes different pandemics and countries with diverse institutional and political backgrounds. Furthermore, it only contemplates "safe assets" in the analysis. In integrated financial markets, this is not an issue since returns should equalize across all asset types. However, financial integration was uncommon in pre-industrialized economies, and the sovereign debt interest rates could diverge from other asset returns. Given these caveats, we expect that pandemic-related mortality reduces real returns in the Malthusian framework presented before. These are precisely the findings of Jordà et al. (2021), which interpret their results along the same lines.

Other authors have found similar declines in the real return of capital, but they have not attributed this decline to the Black Death. Stasavage (2016) argues that institutional changes caused the fall in interest rates paid by government debt of city-states and territorial states. Clark (2008) ascribes the persistence in England of the low return assets after the Black Death to modifications in the time preferences of the population. Finally, Schmelzing (2020) rejects that the Black Death caused a decline in interest rates. On the contrary, he argues that this pandemic interrupted a long-term trend towards lower interest rates.

To summarize, even though the empirical evidence on the effect of pre-industrialized pandemics on the returns to assets is inconclusive, the suggestive and indirect evidence is consistent with the Malthusian prediction derived above. Pre-industrialized pandemics increased the land/labour ratio, which pushed down the returns to land. We now turn to the effects of the Spanish Flu on housing.

Modern Pandemics and Housing

In this section, we develop a simple framework to understand the effects of modern pandemics on housing. After deriving the model predictions, we will explain the consequences of the Spanish Flu. We will focus this discussion on the Spanish case, from which we gathered information on the housing market.

The previous discussion on the returns to land in a Malthusian economy no longer applies to modern economies because most of its assets are reproducible. As we mentioned earlier, we focus our discussion on housing since it was the most important physical asset in the Spanish economy of the early twentieth century (Prados de la Escosura and Rosés, 2009). We characterize the housing market with the following two equations,

$$HS : H = H^S(p, c, \varepsilon, K) \qquad (5.4)$$

$$HD : H = H^D(p.w, R, L) \qquad (5.5)$$

Equation 5.4 is the aggregate housing supply, which may depend on four elements: (i) prices (p), (ii) construction costs (c), (iii) the housing supply elasticity (ε), and (iv) the capital of developers (K). The housing supply depends positively on the price. Once the price increases, developers increase the stock of housing in the country. Increases in construction costs contribute to a decrease of the housing supply. The construction costs depend on a series of factors: the price of land available for development, construction workers' wages, construction materials prices, and technology. Housing supply elasticity determines the slope of the housing supply. One important determinant of the housing supply elasticity is the land available to build new houses. If there is no more development land, the housing stock remains constant, and it does not react to changes in prices. If there is land available for development, the housing stock will increase fast with prices. Developers also need funds (capital) to construct new houses. Sometimes this capital is obtained with credits from the financial sector. Then, when funds for new developments are abundant, the housing supply increases.

Equation 5.5 is the aggregate housing demand. This housing demand may depend on different factors. We consider that it mainly depends on four elements: (i) price (p), (ii) wages or net family income (w), (iii) interest rate (R), and (iv) population (L). The demand for housing should depend negatively on prices.[7] If net family income goes down, households will demand a smaller house (or will prefer the renting option) and, thus, aggregate housing demand will decrease. The third element is the interest rate (or the return on safe assets). We expect the interest rate to affect housing demand negatively. There are, at least, two reasons to think that this is the case. First, if the cost of borrowing decreases, the housing demand will increase. Second, for people who think of housing as an investment, if the return of government bonds declines, the desire to invest in other assets will increase. Lastly, the fourth element that determines aggregate housing demand is the size of the population, particularly the formation of new families. Housing demand increases with population growth. A variant of this situation happens during the structural change when many families decide to change their location. Then, the population in agricultural localities decrease while growing in industrial ones. That is, housing demand will shift within the country (region).

Which will be the effect of the pandemic on the housing market? Point 0 in Fig. 5.1 represents the initial equilibrium. Note that point 0 is where housing demand and supply intersect. We do not think that a pandemic will change the housing supply curve in the long run. That is, the land available to build new houses will not change overnight. However, the pandemic can affect the supply curve in the short run. If the pandemic has a substantial impact on the workforce or/and disrupt the supply of

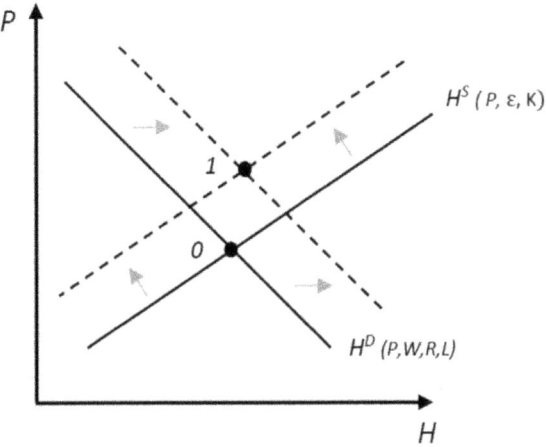

Fig. 5.1 Theoretical effect of pandemics on the housing market (*Notes* Graphical summary of the effects of pandemics on the housing market. $H^S[.]$ and $H^S[.]$ stand for housing supply and demand, respectively. Dots represent the aggregate equilibrium in the housing market for the different assumptions made in the text.)

construction materials, the construction of new houses can stop. If there is intense competition for scarce labour due to high mortality, construction workers' wages can grow, thereby raising construction costs and reducing housing supply. Finally, developers may react to the pandemic. For example, developers may choose to build houses in the less-affected regions and, thus, flee the most devastated areas. Note that construction funds (in contrast to land and housing) can move across places. This supply reallocation could have two main reasons. First, developers in regions with higher mortality can have more problems with workforce recruitment. Second, due to the spatial differences in mortality, vacant houses and housing demand might shrink more in some regions than others. In this sense, the Spanish flu mortality was higher among young adults (see Chapter 3), the most important demographic group for housing demand.

The housing demand may change in different directions too. According to what we have discussed in Chapter 4, real wages decline in modern pandemics, and this could push down demand. On the other hand, we have also discussed in this chapter that interest rates tend to decrease during pandemics. Subsequently, this could propel housing demand.

In sum, as the reader may notice, the direction of the change in housing demand and supply is theoretically ambiguous. Figure 5.1 represents a hypothetical case where a modern pandemic increases housing demand and simultaneously decreases supply. In this case, house prices increase with the pandemic (the equilibrium moves from point 0 to point 1).

The 1918 Flu and Housing: Evidence from Spain

We are now ready to review the Spanish Flu impact on the housing market. We focus this section on the Spanish case. To the best of our knowledge, there are no other similar exercises for other countries at the time of the writing of this book. As we have discussed in Chapter 4, Spain is an ideal country to investigate the effect of flu. We divide this section into two parts. First, we will explain the consequences of the flu on house prices. Then, we will discuss the effect of the flu on the Spanish credit market.

Before proceeding further is important to review some of the main characteristics of Spanish housing markets during the first third of the twentieth century since it exhibited some stark differences with contemporary housing markets.[8] All are highly pertinent for this analysis. First, contrary to today's markets, homeownership was not pervasive, but most families rented their homes. Second, the supply of housing was elastic. Third, government market intervention was minimal. And, finally, mortgages were for businesses and not for first-time buyers.

The absence of widespread homeownership had institutional roots. The Spanish property law before 1960 did not allow independent ownership of land and the buildings constructed on it. Given that the tendency in Spain was to build apartment buildings, this made it impossible for the families to get into housing property. Therefore, specialized landowners took the Spanish housing market.

The elasticity of the housing supply was not only related to the Spanish housing market institutions but also to the infrastructure policy of the local administrations. Housing regulation was very liberal, which allowed the continuous expansion of new buildings. Spanish cities developed zoning plans during the nineteenth century, but they became obsolete due to the rapid population growth. However, Spanish law did not limit housing construction outside the zoning requirement. So, Spanish cities expanded in the suburbs, albeit some densification also took place. Massive public investments in public infrastructures (urban transport, sanitation, streets, secondary roads, water, electricity, and communications) facilitated this spatial expansion, increasing the housing supply elasticity.

Excluding its role in infrastructure development and the protection of property rights, the Spanish authorities intervened little in the market. In particular, the number of houses developed or owned by public authorities was limited. Furthermore, in sharp contrast with other European countries, the government did not regulate the rent market's conditions, and rent controls were not implemented in Spain after World War I.

The relationship between credit and housing markets differed strongly from today's practices. Foremost, first-time buyers did not have mortgages since there was only business credit. Many mortgages were employed to support different kinds of businesses and were not used exclusively in housing development. The banks, and other credit institutions, did not monopolize this market. The most important institution, the Banco Hipotecario de España (The Mortgage Bank of Spain), lent about 9% of mortgages in 1918 and 11% in 1921.[9] Therefore, most of the mortgage lenders were individuals. The loan-to-value ratio was low, typically 50% or less. The average value of mortgaged properties also surpassed the average property price. So, credit access was constrained. Finally, the mortgage market was less homogenous than today. Mortgage maturity went from one to 50 years, and interest rates could diverge substantially from the preferential interest rate. In this sense, the riskier mortgages could pay rates above 6%, while the safer ones paid about 4% or less.

We examine the effect of the Spanish Flu on house prices in Spain. The empirical strategy is like the one discussed for real wages in Chapter 4. That is, we exploit within-country differences in excess mortality to identify the causal effect of the Spanish Flu. Thus, we employ the following specification,

$$\Delta Y_{ct} = \beta_t \sum_{t=t_c}^{T} Flu_c \, D_t + \gamma Y_{ct-1} + \delta_c + \delta_t + \varepsilon_{ct'} \qquad (5.6)$$

where ΔY_{ct} is annual growth rate of real house prices, Y_{ct} is (log) real house price in province c in year t, Flu_c is excess mortality during the Spanish Flu (the year 1918) in province c (as a measure of flu-related mortality), and δ_c and δ_t are province and year fixed effects. D_t is a dummy equal to one for year t and 0 otherwise. The analysis goes from 1915 to 1930. We consider two types of specifications. First, to identify the contemporaneous effect, we consider $D_{1918} = 1$ for year 1918 and $D_{Post-1918} = 1$ for years after 1918. Then, to examine the overall long-run effect of the Spanish Flu, we assume $D_{Post-1917} = 1$ for years after 1917 and 0 otherwise. Note that β inform us on whether provinces with more excess mortality during the Spanish Flu had higher housing price growth during (after) the Spanish Flu.

We use two measures of real house prices: with and without hedonic adjustment. Table 5.1 reproduces the estimated coefficients.

These estimates show that the effect of the Spanish Flu on house prices was positive. Prominently, the shock effect seems to build over time and had some persistence. Indeed, whereas the evidence on the contemporaneous effect is mixed, the long-run one (up to 1930) is positive ($\beta_{post-1917} > 0$ and $\beta_{post-1918} > 0$). It implies that, compared to pre-1918, house prices increased more in provinces with more flu-related mortality. Quantitatively, the long-run effect is small compared with the analogous results for real wages. For example, in the case of hedonic prices, a 1% increase in flu mortality translates into an increase in roughly

Table 5.1 Effects of the flu on urban house prices in Spain

	(1) No Hedonic	(2) Hedonic
Panel A: Short-run effects		
$Flu1918_c * D_{1918}$	4.39	1.54**
	(5.50)	(0.71)
$Flu1918c * D_{Post-1918}$	24.22***	3.16***
	(6.68)	(0.75)
Lag Real Rent$_{ct}$	−0.97***	−0.85***
	(0.08)	(0.09)
Panel B: Long-run effects		
$Flu1918c * D_{Post-1917}$	22.65**	3.02***
	(6.76)	(0.77)
Lag real Rent$_{ct}$	−0.96***	−0.85***
	(0.09)	(0.09)
Province fixed effects	Y	Y
Year fixed effects	Y	Y
Observations	720	720

Notes The dependent variable is the annual growth rate of real housing prices for province and year. The hedonic prices are regression-adjusted housing prices. House price data drawn from Carmona et al. (2014, 2017). See Table 4.1 for information on estimation methods. *p < 0.10, **p < 0.05, ***p < 0.01

3% in house prices. For real wages, the contemporaneous negative effect for agricultural workers was six times bigger. In any event, we want to emphasize that the adjustment in the labour and housing market was very different.

At this point of our research, we cannot offer a definitive explanation of the reasons behind this housing market behaviour during the 1918 flu. However, we will use the previous theoretical framework to advance some plausible explanations.

First, let us focus on housing demand. We know that real wages declined, and this change was permanent in several occupations. We also know that wages took time to recover from the initial loss. Furthermore, according to Eq. 5.5, provinces with more flu-related mortality (and hence less population) should demand fewer new houses. Consequently, housing demand, and prices, should decline due to the income and population shocks. However, Table 5.1. suggests that this channel was not driving the results.

A second possibility, which we cannot test with the available historical data, is a composition effect in housing demand. It could be that in provinces with more flu-related mortality, only the wealthy people purchased houses. Since higher quality houses were more expensive than the average ones, the overall aggregate house price increased. This phenomenon could happen in the short run, but it is a stretch to think that the compositional shock could last for a decade.

A third demand-related hypothesis is that internal migration from rural to urban locations was higher in provinces with more flu-related mortality. This migration shock could increase (urban) housing demand and push up housing prices. However, this migration push had likely been counterbalanced by the population leaving these same provinces. In any case, sparse evidence gives little support to this internal migration hypothesis. From 1920 to 1930, urbanization rate growth was higher among the less flu-affected provinces. Simultaneously, they also attracted migrants from the provinces with the highest flu-related mortality rates.

Let us now move to a housing supply interpretation. A plausible outcome of the 1918 flu was that some provinces had problems recruiting construction workers, and house construction had to stop. This labour scarcity could increase housing prices due to its impact on housing costs. However, this phenomenon only had a short-term effect since the Spanish labour market for semiskilled and unskilled workers was elastic and flexible during this period. Therefore, if there was some labour scarcity of construction workers, this could be easily solved by reallocating labour from other sectors or/and migration from other provinces.

As we explained above, another main component of the housing supply is capital. Arguably, it can move easier than labour across sectors and locations. Developers do not need to move their housing projects from their preferred location but can invest in other developers' initiatives outside their initial business location. Furthermore, capital for housing construction can also migrate when mortgage lenders decide to change the location of their construction credits. In the case of housing, a strong constraint for the fast movement of capital is information on construction opportunities in different locations. The spatial distortions caused by zoning and other regulations exacerbate this problem. However, as we noted above, the land supply for new developments was elastic in Spain during the first third of the twentieth century. Hence, market distortions were likely to be less important than today.

Was it rational for investors, and lenders, to move capital outside the regions most affected by the pandemic? If they thought that the housing demand shock was permanent, the answer is yes. The evidence indicates that the flu shock was permanent since mortality was the highest among young adults, the most important demographic group for housing demand. If this were the case, we could explain why flu-related mortality was associated with increases in house prices.

In sum, we argue that the Spanish Flu was conducive to a reallocation of capital away from the regions with more flu-related mortality towards those with less mortality. In addition, this capital reallocation could be more intense for urban than for rural risk capital.

Our initial results are consistent with this interpretation. Figure 5.2 reports suggestive evidence. Panel A presents the evolution of aggregate urban and rural credit in Spain. Before the Spanish Flu, the trend of both measures was negative and similar. However, there was a trend break shortly after the Spanish Flu (around 1919). Trends became positive, but the slope of urban credit was higher. Spain was booming in the 1920s, but urban credit growth was impressive. Indeed, annual GDP grew at an average of 4% during the decade, but urban credit grew at 23% over the same period. To put this number into perspective, during the recent housing (debt) bubble, Spanish household and corporate credits grew at 25% in the peak (2004) but not in the previous and subsequent years. The counterpart peak in the United States was 10%.[10] We do not attempt to link this increase in overall credit to the Spanish Flu. We argue that this credit, especially the riskier urban one, was channelled disproportionally towards provinces with less flu-related mortality. Moreover, consistently with our hypothesis, the increase in urban credit was steeper than the rural one since cities had lower 1918 flu-mortality rates than the countryside.

Panel b provides more direct evidence of our hypothesis. It reports the evolution of the urban riskier credit for provinces in the top (orange) and bottom (blue) quartile of the flu-related mortality distribution. It is apparent from the figure that the trend on this type of urban credit was similar in both regional groups before the pandemic, specifically between 1915 and 1918. However, after the Spanish Flu, trends are no longer parallel, and credit increased disproportionately more in provinces with low flu-related mortality (blue line). Pre-1918, urban riskier credit declined by 21% in low flu-related mortality provinces and 22% in

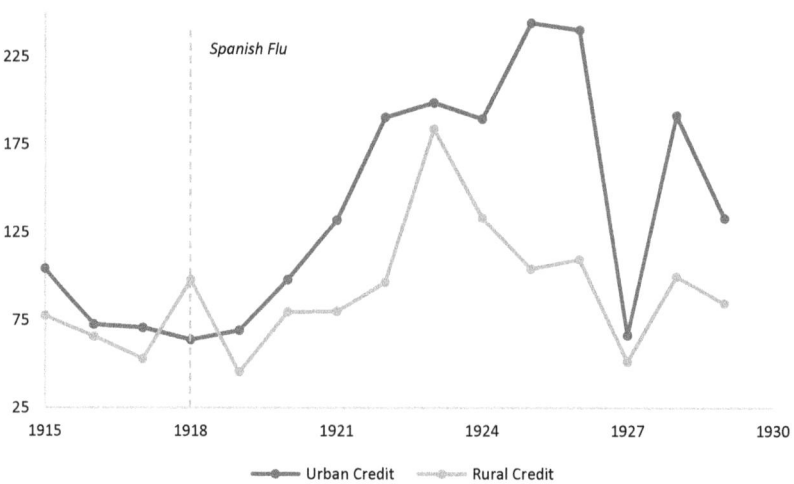

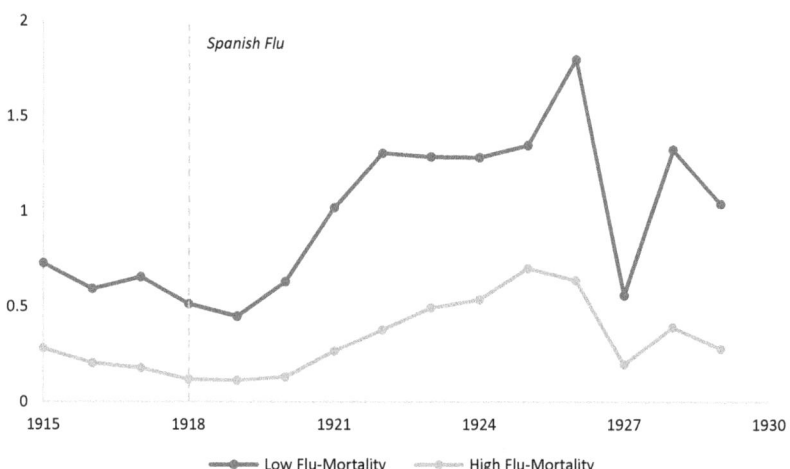

Fig. 5.2 Effect of the flu on mortgage markets in Spain (*Notes* Panel **a**. reports the evolution of total urban [rural] mortgage credit in real terms. Panel **b**. reports the evolution of risk urban credit in the province in the top and bottom quartile of the flu-mortality distribution. Risk credit is a mortgage credit at an interest rate above 6%. See Basco et al. [2021] for details.)

high flu-related mortality ones. Instead, between 1918 and 1925, urban credit increased 83% in the low flu-related mortality provinces and only 58% in the high flu-related mortality ones. Thus, according to these numbers, flu-related excess mortality decreased urban credit by roughly 23% (the difference in growth between the two groups before and after the shock).

To conclude, if this evidence on capital movements is correct, we can infer that the impact of the pandemic was more significant than previously thought. More prominently, it means that pandemics can have persistent effects due to the spatial reallocation of capital. In our case, capital was being reallocated towards urbanized regions, which had experienced low flu-related mortality. This capital reallocation was likely less relevant in pre-industrialized economies since the most important asset (land) was immobile. In our case, one could argue that the Spanish Flu helped to industrialize (urbanize) regions with low flu-related mortality. A similar feature may already be occurring with the emergence of Covid-19. Labour and housing demand (capital) is moving outside the high-density regions in the United States and England.[11] Thus, this current reallocation could also have permanent effects and change capital location and, arguably, reduce regional productivity differences.

NOTES

1. Therefore, we use an ampler definition of capital than those commonly used in national accounting and productivity studies (for example, we include land in the definition). In these frameworks (Prados de la Escosura & Rosés, 2010), the stock of capital is commonly defined as all tangible goods that can be used during more than one period to produce other goods and services. More specifically, the capital stock comprises residential and non-residential structures, transport equipment, and machinery. Consequently, intangible goods (like licenses, patents, and property rights), nonreproducible goods (like monuments, pieces of art, and natural resources, including land), consumer durables, military goods, inventories, and intermediate products are not part of this capital stock measure.
2. The same situation is also observable in Spain during the period of this pandemic. The most important component of the capital stock was housing, while the relative importance of land was rapidly decreasing. The interested reader could consult the detailed account of Prados de la Escosura and Rosés (2009, 2010).

3. See Basco (2018) for a theoretical and empirical review.
4. However, there is a large family of production functions that also feature these two properties. Thus, our theoretical predictions will extend to most production functions. We need some elasticity of substitution between inputs, but it does not need to be one. In other words, we could have employed a more general production function like a CES (constant elasticity of substitution).
5. One exception to this finding for the Black Death was Spain (Álvarez Nogal et al., 2021). Interestingly, they document that the ratio between wages and return to land (w/R) declined. This a surprising finding because, according to Eq. 5.2, it would imply that the Black Death decreased the amount of land per capita. Since this is highly unlikely, it must be the case that either Spain did not feature these Malthusian characteristics or that other institutional factors reacted.
6. Alfani (2022) reviews the recent evidence on changes in wealth distribution during the Black Death. Studies with data from several cities in Italian, France, Spain, and Germany show that the Gini coefficient decreased after the Black Death. For example, in the Italian Prato, the Gini coefficient decreased from 0.7 to 0.5.
7. It may be the case that for some segments of the housing market (luxury homes), larger prices increase demand. However, for the average (representative) house, the slope will be negative.
8. This review of the Spanish housing markets characteristics is based on Carmona at al. (2014, 2017).
9. On this public bank role on the Spanish mortgage market, see Lacomba et al. (1990).
10. See Basco (2018) for more details on the recent housing bubble.
11. This is a recent phenomenon and there is still substantial uncertainty about its causes and consequences. See, among others, Cheshire et al. (2021), D'Lima et al. (2021), Gallent and Madeddu (2021), Lee and Huang (2022), and McCord et al. (2022).

References

Alfani, G. (2015). Economic inequality in Northwestern Italy: A long-term view (fourteenth to eighteenth centuries). *Journal of Economic History, 75*(4), 1058–1096.

Alfani, G. (2022). Epidemics, inequality, and poverty in preindustrial and early industrial times. *Journal of Economic Literature, 60*(1), 3–40.

Álvarez Nogal, C., Prados de la Escosura, L., & Santiago Caballero, C. (2021). *Economic effects of the Black Death: Spain in European perspective* (Instituto Figuerola Working Papers in Economic History, 2020-06).

Basco, S. (2018). *Housing bubbles*. Palgrave Macmillan.
Basco, S., Domènech, J., & Rosés, J. R. (2021). Capital market, mortgage credit and pandemics: Evidence from the Spanish Flu. mimeo.
Carmona, J., Lampe, M., & Rosés, J. R. (2014). Spanish housing markets, 1904–1934: New evidence. *Revista De Historia Económica/Journal of Iberian and Latin American Economic History, 32*(1), 119–150.
Carmona, J., Lampe, M., & Rosés, J. (2017). Housing affordability during the urban transition in Spain. *The Economic History Review, 70*(2), 632–658.
Cheshire, P., Hilber, C., & Schöni, O. (2021). *The pandemic and the housing market: A British story* (CEP Covid-19 Papers, 020).
Clark, G. (2008). *A farewell to Alms*. Princeton University Press.
D'Lima, W., Lopez, L. A., & Pradhan, A. (2021). COVID-19 and housing market effects: Evidence from us shutdown orders. *Real Estate Economics*, forthcoming.
Gallent, N., & Madeddu, M. (2021). Covid-19 and London's decentralising housing market—What are the planning implications? *Planning Practice and Research, 36*(5), 567–577.
Jordà, Ò., Knoll, K., Kuvshinov, D., Schularick, M., & Taylor, A. M. (2019). The rate of return on everything, 1870–2015. *Quarterly Journal of Economics, 134*, 1225–1298.
Jordà, Ò., Singh, S. R., & Taylor, A. M. (2021). Longer-run economic consequences of pandemics. *Review of Economics and Statistics*, forthcoming.
Lacomba, J. A., Ruiz, G., de la Macorra, L., & Ruiz, A. (1990). *Una historia del Banco Hipotecario de España*. Alianza Editorial.
Lee, J., & Huang, Y. (2022). Covid-19 impact on US housing markets: Evidence from spatial regression models. *Spatial Economic Analysis*, forthcoming.
McCord, M., Lo, D., McCord, J., Davis, P., Haran, M., & Turley, P. (2022). The impact of COVID-19 on house prices in Northern Ireland: Price persistence, yet divergent? *Journal of Property Research*, forthcoming.
Prados, L., & Rosés, J. R. (2009). The sources of long-run growth in Spain, 1850–2000. *Journal of Economic History, 69*(4), 1063–1091.
Prados, L., & Rosés, J. R. (2010). Long-run estimates of physical capital in Spain, 1850–2000. *Research in Economic History, 27*, 141–200.
Schmelzing, P. (2020). *Eight centuries of global real rates, R-G, and the 'suprasecular' decline, 1311–2018* (Staff Working Papers, 845). Bank of England.
Stasavage, D. (2016). What we can learn from the early history of sovereign debt. *Explorations in Economic History, 59*(supp. C), 1–16.

CHAPTER 6

Taking Stock: The Aggregate Effects of the Spanish Flu

Abstract Do pandemics affect the aggregate production of the economy? If this is the case, are the effects long-lived? To consider these two questions, we propose a framework to understand the effects of pandemics on short- and long-run aggregate output. We review the diverse economic consequences of pre-world pandemics (including the Black Death) and the Spanish Flu. Finally, we explain how the Spanish Flu can help us consider the potential unequal economic effects of Covid-19.

Keyword AS-AD model · Aggregate output · Persistence · Pandemics · Covid-19

Aggregate Effects of Pandemics

We have reached the end of our journey on the economic effects of pandemics. We have discussed the disparate results of pandemics on mortality, labour (wages), and capital markets (housing). However, we should not conclude this book without a discussion of the potential consequences of pandemics on the aggregate economy. Is GDP affected by pandemics? How persistent are the potential effects? To answer these substantial questions, we will, first, discuss the predictions of standard macroeconomic theory and then we will review the existing empirical evidence.

The AS-AD model (aggregate supply-aggregate demand) is the standard macroeconomic model to understand what determines aggregate output and prices in equilibrium. Employing this model, we will briefly discuss how pandemics may differently affect the short- and long-run equilibrium. It is beyond this book's scope to give micro-foundations to this model components. We refer the interested reader to any intermediate macroeconomic textbook.

We start with the short-run predictions of the effects of pandemics on aggregate output, later we will consider its long-run forecasts. The following two equations summarize the AS-AD model,

$$AD: Y = f_D(P) \qquad (6.1)$$

$$AS: Y = f_S(P) \qquad (6.2)$$

Equation 6.1 represents aggregate demand. The components of aggregate demand are consumption, investment, government spending, and the current account (export minus imports). Aggregate demand decreases with prices (i.e., $f'_D(P) < 0$). To understand this relationship, we can employ households' microeconomics. Given their disposable income, households will decide to purchase fewer goods when prices rise. An increase in prices also affects investment through the effect of real money balances on interest rates. The mechanism is the following. When prices increase, the real money balances decline.[1] It raises the equilibrium interest in the money market, thereby decreasing overall investment. On the other hand, aggregate demand can also decline when the propensity to consume (share of income devoted to purchasing goods) or invest declines. For example, when there is uncertainty about future income, households decide to save more and/or firms decide to cut investment.

Equation 6.2 is the aggregate supply. As its name indicates, aggregate supply is the total output that the economy produces. Its main components are productivity, capital (and land), and employment (hours worked). The literature disagrees about the slope of the aggregate supply curve in the short run. The "classical view" is that this curve is vertical. It implies that prices are fully flexible, and firms will react by charging higher prices once they observe demand changes. Firms will not adjust their labour demand and, thus, production will remain constant. Instead, in the "Keynesian view", prices are not flexible. So, if the demand for goods declines, firms cannot cut their prices. Therefore, firms will fire workers (or reduce hours worked) and lower production to avoid negative profits.

However, most economists now agree that the slope of the aggregate supply is positive (i.e., $f'_S(P) > 0$) in the short run. The supply curve is positive because prices are neither completely fixed nor fully flexible but in-between (sticky prices) in the short run. Economists have used models with menu costs to micro-founded sticky prices. The foundation of these models is that firms are hesitant to post new prices due to the cost incurred. So, firms will modify prices only when there is a substantial mismatch between the "optimal" (desired) price and the actual price. Subsequently, the aggregate equilibrium in the short run is given by,

$$Y^* = f_D(P^*) = f_S(P^*) \qquad (6.3)$$

This short-run equilibrium is represented graphically in Panel A of Fig. 6.1. As discussed above, aggregate supply (AS) is upward sloping, and aggregate demand (AD) is downward sloping. The equilibrium, where

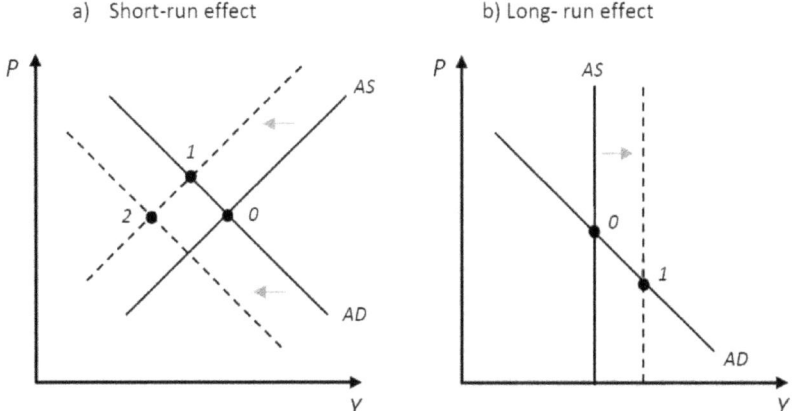

Fig. 6.1 Theoretical effect of pandemics on aggregate output (*Notes* Graphical summary of the short- and long-run effects of pandemics on aggregate output. AS and AD stand for aggregate supply and aggregate demand, respectively. Dots represent the aggregate equilibrium in the goods market for the different assumptions made in the text)

the two curves meet, is point 0. At this point, aggregate supply is equal to aggregate demand. Employing this framework, we can discuss the short-run effects of pandemics.

How do pandemics affect the aggregate supply and aggregate demand curves in the short run? Let us start with the aggregate supply. Every pandemic is associated with an increase in sick people and a sizeable spike in mortality rates. The sick workers have less productivity, which is akin to reducing the number of working hours per worker. Moreover, if workers are aware of the pandemic, they may refuse to work.[2] In sum, pandemics lead to reductions in hours worked. So, the aggregate supply curve will shift to the left. If this is the only pandemic effect, the new equilibrium would be at point 1. There is less output at higher prices given fewer goods produced, and demand has not changed. Productivity also remains unaffected in the short run.

We consider straight away the effect of the pandemics on aggregate demand in the short run. The first obvious outcome is that mortality rises reduce aggregate demand. However, no matter how impressive the mortality may be, aggregate consumption changes are likely determined

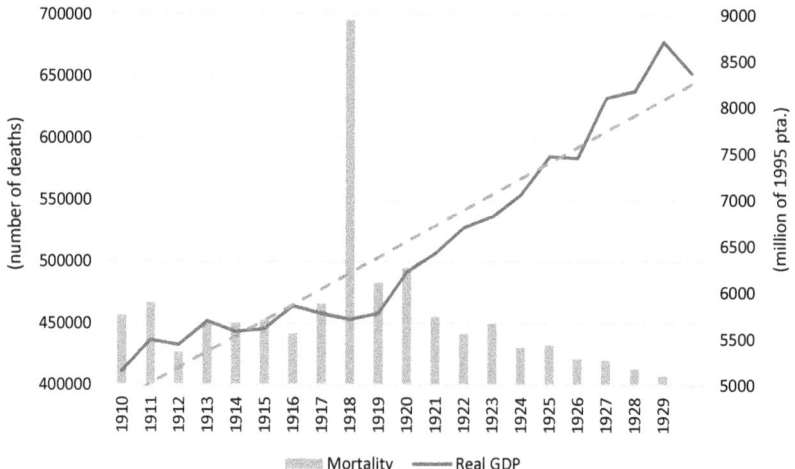

Fig. 6.2 Aggregate effect of the flu in Spain (*Notes* The blue bar reports the evolution of annual deaths in Spain and the orange line reports the real GDP. For death data see Chapter 3, and Gross Domestic Product [GDP] in 1995 constant prices obtained from Prados de la Escosura [2017])

by surviving households and individuals' behaviour. For example, sick people tend to consume less and save more, and healthy people can also increase savings because of doubts about future health and income. Similarly, firms can also cut investments due to demand uncertainty or anticipating potential input and labour bottlenecks. In this sense, a substantial literature has shown that uncertainty escalations reduce investment, depressing the whole economy.[3] Once again, the importance of this demand effect is contingent on the economy's characteristics. For example, if we compare a Malthusian (agricultural) economy with the industrialized one, the demand effect is stronger in the latter than in the former. In hand-to-mouth societies, the option of deferring consumption is not available. As reproduced in Fig. 6.1, panel A, pandemics shift down aggregate demand and reduce equilibrium prices and output.

In sum, we conclude that pandemics affect aggregate output (and prices) in the short run through both supply and demand. Point 2, panel A, reproduces a potential final short-run equilibrium. In this case, output declines, and the effect on prices is uncertain. If the demand effect dominates, pandemics will be associated with deflation. If the supply effect dominates, pandemics will be conducive to inflation. The consequences of the pandemics on output per capita are also ambiguous: output per capita may rise in the short run if the decline in population offsets the output reduction.

How do pandemics affect long-run aggregate output? Aggregate demand can fall in the short run because households and firms become more risk-averse and moderate consumption. However, we think that this risk aversion is unlikely to affect several generations.[4] Another possible impact of the pandemics is a permanent structural change in the composition of demand. For example, Pamuk (2007) argues that the Black Death was responsible for a reallocation of demand from essential goods and necessities towards goods with higher income elasticity. However, it is unclear if this new demand pattern was the source of the long-run changes in the economy or a direct consequence of the higher incomes (productivity) caused by a supply shift.

Instead, a change in the long-run aggregate supply (AS) is a more likely effect of a pandemic. In the long run, the economy is at full potential using all available economic resources and, hence, aggregate supply does not depend on prices.[5] So, the stock of capital, the stock of land, and population (workforce) are fully employed. Consequently, long-run aggregate supply shifts are mainly consequences of changes in aggregate productivity.[6]

There are several channels for this pandemic-related productivity shift. Pandemics could encourage the development of innovations that can increase aggregate productivity. One possibility is that they increased technological change. Catastrophic mortality boosts the cost of labour, which give incentives to firms to create new (labour-saving) technologies, thereby increasing the long-run potential output of the economy (Acemoglu, 2002). Another possibility is that pandemics encourage the adoption of better institutions.[7] The pandemics alter the relationship among the factors of production and can cause social conflict. If this social conflict leads to political change and better institutions, we expect a long-run aggregate supply increase (Acemoglu et al., 2005).

Panel B in Fig. 6.1 reproduces the long-run effects of pandemics. Note that the long-run aggregate supply shifts to the right and, thus, the equilibrium moves from point 0 to point 1. In this new long-run equilibrium, aggregate output is higher, and prices are lower than before the pandemic. Therefore, the pandemic has positive long-run effects in this case.

What Have We Learnt from Past Pandemics?

We review the empirical evidence on the short- and long-run economic effects of pandemics in this section. We divide this discussion into two parts. Analogously to the chapter on the labour market (Chapter 4), the narrative starts with pre-industrial pandemics and finish with the Spanish Flu.

Pandemics in the Pre-industrial World

The Black Death has been the most devastating pandemic of history (see Chapter 1). The analysis of this mortality disaster has shaped how economists think about the effects of pandemics on the aggregate economy. However, the experience of the Black Death is hardly representative of what happened in other pre-modern and modern pandemics.

There is a consensus that the short-run economic effects of deadly pandemics in the pre-industrial economies were substantial. Alfani and Murphy (2017) explain how pre-modern pandemics disrupted economic activity. They also led to the destruction of human and physical capital. Even though it is impossible to quantify the relative importance of the supply and demand effects, a fall in supply was arguably the most relevant channel through which pre-industrial pandemics affected aggregate output in the short run. Following the reasoning of the theory above, if the supply effect led to output contraction, prices should grow. Even though data on aggregate prices is rare, there is suggestive evidence during the Black Death consistent with this prediction (Jedwab et al., 2021).

Regarding the short-term evolution of income, GDP per capita can increase if the decline in population offsets the fall in output because of the Black Death. In an agrarian (Malthusian) economy, this is the expected result of a negative demographic shock since the stock of land remained intact. England and Northern Italy (Broadberry, 2021) experienced this process of income growth. However, this was not the case in Spain (Alvarez Nogal et al., 2021), where GDP per capita decreased. The explanation for this exception is that the market disruption caused by the Black Death was so intense that the surviving population could not take advantage of the new abundance of natural resources and land.[8]

The effects of the Black Death, in the long run, were heterogeneous. The initial short-term income gains remained in Northwestern Europe after the population recovery. More prominently, economic growth accelerated slowly until industrialization.[9] Voigtländer and Voth (2013) argue that the Black Death was the shock (along with wars and other pandemics) that permanently increased real wages and enabled western countries to industrialize. Instead, these income gains disappeared in South and Eastern Europe once the population reached pre-pandemic levels.

There is no consensus on the causes of these stark differences in economic growth after the plague.[10] Research has sometimes associated the growth failure of eastern Europe with a deterioration of institutions because of the Black Death. Contrary to Western Europe, where the Black Death ravaged feudal institutions, Eastern Europe experienced their intensification (the "second serfdom").[11]

Beyond the Black Death, the pandemics growth effects seem to be country dependent. So, the picture presented in Alfani and Murphy (2017) for other pre-industrialized world pandemics is darker. Indeed, they argue that negative long-run effects seem the rule more than the exception. For example, they discuss evidence on seventeenth-century plagues in Southern Europe, which may have contributed to a North–South Europe divergence. In addition, Harper (2016) also shows that ancient plagues in Roman Egypt had long-run adverse effects.

The Spanish Flu

We now turn to the Spanish Flu. Before the emergence of Covid-19, there was little research about the economic effects of the Spanish Flu. However, the outburst of Covid-19 cases has increased the interest in this pandemic, and we have now several studies about its economic effects.[12]

Two main dimensions distinguish the empirical literature on the economic effects of the Spanish Flu. First, research differs on the nature of spatial units considered. Some papers exploit mortality differences across countries, whereas others review differences across regions within a country. There are advantages and problems in both options. For example, some countries have few administrative units, making it impossible to compute reliable statistical results. At the same time, when comparing very different countries, there is the risk of not having a credible control group and comparing pears with apples. Second, papers differed on the measure of flu-related mortality. As explained in Chapter 3, an excess mortality measure of flu-related mortality has considerable methodological advantages over the alternatives. However, it is impossible to use this methodology in countries involved in World War I. Therefore, research on belligerent countries has employed the causes collected in death certificates. So, flu-related mortality figures are not fully comparable among different countries, being higher and more reliable where excess mortality methodology is employed.

Which was the short-run effect of the Spanish Flu? Barro et al. (2020) examine the impact of flu-related mortality on GDP per capita across 48 countries. They find that the Spanish Flu worsened GDP per capita by around 6% in the mean-affected country.[13] The recent study of De Santis and Van der Veken (2020) found a substantial variation of the impact of the pandemic across countries affecting disproportionately lower-income countries. Specifically, their estimated GDP loss from 1918 to 1920 due to the pandemic is twice as large for lower-income countries (9.8%) than for higher-income countries (4.7%).

The presence of two confounded disturbances hampers country studies of the economic impact of the 1918 flu. In belligerent countries, GDP was directly affected by the Great War and the related interventionist government policies. Furthermore, all countries, even those that were neutral, experienced the economic consequences of the conflict on international trade and finance. However, the results of the available country studies do not differ substantially from the cross-country study of Barro et al. (2020). Italian regions with the highest mortality rates experienced a roughly 6.5% excess decline in GDP relative to ones that experienced the lowest mortality rates (Carillo & Japelli, 2022). In Sweden, the pandemic had a similar negative impact on per capita income: the highest influenza mortality quartile experienced a drop of 5% during the pandemic and an additional 6%afterwards (Karlsson et al., 2014). Danish municipalities most severely affected by flu mortality experienced short-run declines in output of 5% (Dahl et al. 2020). Correia et al. (2020) analyses the impact of the pandemic in the United States. Their results are not directly comparable since they do not have data on GDP per capita. However, they found that the influenza epidemic led to an average 18% reduction in state manufacturing output, but that this disruption was short-lived.[14]

Which was the channel driving the fall in aggregate output? As we have described in the previous section, we need to compute the effect of the pandemic on prices to assess the relative importance of the demand and supply channels. There is not much evidence on consumer prices. Barro et al. (2020) introduce inflation as an outcome variable in their cross-country analysis. As the same authors recognize, belligerent countries' price controls influenced the reported price data. It is, thus, difficult not to take with a grain of salt their result that the Spanish Flu temporary increased inflation.

The sparse evidence also indicates that this decline in production was not homogeneous across sectors and points to the presence of the demand channel. For the United States, Velde (2020) found that industrial output fell sharply but rebounded within months. Instead, retail, and financial sectors were little affected. In one interesting case study, Gallardo-Albarrán and de Zwart (2021) fail to obtain a negative effect of flu-related mortality on sugar production in Indonesia. These findings for sugar production in Indonesia contrast with the fall in textile production documented in Japan (Noy et al., 2020). As Gallardo-Albarrán and de Zwart discuss, a reallocation of resources towards food production to prevent famine could have taken place. However, it may also be that the decline in demand was more intense for textile products than for food.

We now turn to the potential long-run economic effect of the pandemic. Most of the economic literature has focused on the United States. In this case, the consensus is that the Spanish Flu had a mild short-run negative effect and a null long-run effect on aggregate output. For example, Velde (2020) uses different high-frequency disaggregated data to confirm this point. Benmelech and Frydman (2020) argue that the main reason for this mild contemporaneous effect was World War

I. The war-related demand was so strong that social distance measures, where encouraged, did not affect aggregate demand. Velde (2020) argues that the 1918–19 recession can be attributed more to the Armistice than the pandemic. There was no long-run effect in Italy (Carillo & Japelli, 2022). One could wonder whether this is due to the war efforts. All in all, the emerging consensus is that the Spanish Flu generated a V-shaped recession with moderate negative growth rates in the short run and full recovery after 2 or 3 years.

As argued throughout the book, Spain is an ideal country to identify the effect of the pandemic. Figure 6.2 reports the evolution of GDP and mortality between 1910 and 1930. The peak in mortality (1918) coincides with a trough in GDP. In addition, note that even though the decline in GDP does not seem dramatic (1%), the difference from the trend is significant (6%). However, the economy recovered rapidly, and Spain enjoyed high growth and industrialization during the 1920s (Prados de la Escosura and Rosés, 2009). Therefore, the Spanish experience fits the international view presented before.

To provide further quantitative evidence on the short and long-run impact of the 1918 flu on GDP, we follow the same procedure as those employed with real wages. So, we employ the following standard differences-in-differences specification:

$$Y_{ct} = \beta_t \sum_{t=t_c}^{T} Flu_c \, D_t + \delta_c + \delta_t + \varepsilon_{ct'} \qquad (6.4)$$

where Y_{ct} is (log) real GDP in province c in year t, Flu_c is excess mortality during the Spanish Flu (the year 1918) in province c (as a measure of flu-related mortality), and δ_c and δ_t are province and year fixed effects. D_t is a dummy equal to one for year (period) t, and 0 otherwise. We have information for rural and urban GDPs from 1915 to 1930.

Panel A in Table 6.1 reports the coefficients on the interaction between the excess death rate in 1918 (Flu 1918) and time dummies. We include separate interactions for 1918 and post-1918. First, we focus on the interaction with the 1918 dummy. Coefficients are not statistically significant for all specifications, except for urban GDP. This negative coefficient implies that one percent increase in flu-related mortality translated into an urban GDP decline in 1918, relative to pre-1918, of 2.8%. Second, to assess the persistence of the shock, we compute the interaction between the excess death rate in 1918 and the post-1918 dummy. Aggregate

Table 6.1 Effects of the flu on output in Spain

	(1) GDP	(2) GDP per capita	(3) Rural GDP	(4) Urban GDP
Panel A: Short-run effects				
$Flu1918_c * D_{1918}$	0.003	1.61	4.4	−2.77***
	(2.13)	(1.84)	(3.27)	(0.63)
$Flu1918c * DPost - 1918$	−6.43**	0.74	7.06*	−5.67***
	(2.64)	(2.02)	(-3.66)	(0.70)
Panel B: Long-run effects				
$Flu1918c * DPost - 1917$	−5.94**	0.8	6.86*	−5.45***
	(2.62)	(2.00)	(3.60)	(0.72)
Province fixed effects	Y	Y	Y	Y
Year fixed effects	Y	Y	Y	Y
Observations	768	768	768	768

Notes The dependent variable is yearly real output. Flu 1918 is the value of excess death in 1918. D_{1918} is a dummy equal to one for the year 1918. D_t is a dummy equal to one for period t and zero otherwise. t = Pre-1918 is omitted from the regressions and it is the control period. See text for more details. The table reports fixed effects regressions weighted by population. Standard errors are clustered at the year level. *$p < 0.10$, **$p < 0.05$, ***$p < 0.01$

GDP decreased, on the average province, but GDP per capita were unaffected. Quantitatively, one percent increase in flu-related deaths caused an average decline in aggregate of GDP of around 6%. We observe that there was an heterogenous effect across sectors. Indeed, whereas the coefficient of urban GDP is negative and significant, the coefficient on rural GDP is positive but mildly significant (only at 10%).[15] Finally, Panel B in Table 6.1. investigates the overall long-run effect of the flu on GDP. To do so, it presents the interaction between the Flu 1918 and the post-1917 dummy. The results confirm those of Panel A. All in all, it seems that the 1918 flu had strong permanent negative effects in the urban GDP and milder (less statistically significant) in aggregate GDP, but it did not cause a fall in overall provincial GDP per capita.[16]

What happened with the supply and demand channels in Spain? We found that urban excess mortality was correlated with consumer prices inflation in cities while having no statistically significant effects in the countryside.[17] We also point to a heterogeneous impact of the pandemic in Spain like those observed in other countries. The evolution of the sectoral composition of country-wide output shows that the drop in industrial and service outputs was much more significant than the limited response of agricultural production. The evidence on real wages also supports this demand channel interpretation.[18] In sum, this evidence and those on sectoral composition are consistent with demand dropping in non-essential goods (like textile goods) and increasing food consumption. This demand shock impacted more urban than rural locations.

To conclude, we discuss the potential long-run effects of pandemics not necessarily linked to aggregate income. A substantial literature has considered the long-run welfare consequences of the pandemic shock for the generations living through it. The seminal paper in this literature is Almond (2006). He compares cohorts in utero during the Spanish Flu with other ones in the United States. He shows that pandemic utero cohorts had worse outcomes in terms of health (higher mortality and physical disability), education and income. Parman (2015) shows that, in the United States, parents reinforced the flu shock by shifting educational investments to healthy children. Hong and Yun (2017) found that foetal exposure substantially deteriorated educational attainment, particularly among those born in provinces severely affected by influenza. Instead, for Sweden, Helgertz and Bengtsson (2019) document that foetal exposure had a modest long-run increase in mortality and no significant effect on socioeconomic outcomes (income and occupational attainment). Finally, for Sao Paulo (Brazil), Guimbeau et al. (2021) find evidence in the opposite direction: the Spanish Flu led to higher long-run human capital (literacy). These authors suggest that natural selection can explain these results, especially in less developed countries with few resources like Brazil at the time of the pandemic.

COVID vs Spanish Flu: A First Assessment

To finish the book, we will discuss how the Spanish Flu experience can help us to understand the potential short- and long-run economic consequences of Covid-19. At the time of writing, there is still considerable uncertainty about the evolution of the Covid-19 pandemic. The health experts do not know whether more waves or new variants of the Covid are on the way and if these new waves will be deadly or not. Due to these high levels of uncertainty, many of our conclusions are necessarily provisional.

Before proceeding with this comparative analysis, it is important to emphasize some substantial differences between the Spanish flu and the Covid-19 pandemic. The Spanish flu was more deadly and affected many more young adults than Covid-19. Furthermore, lockdowns were uncommon, and vaccines were ineffective during the 1918 flu. Finally, it was coetaneous to World War I, and the conflict masked many of its economic consequences.

One main lesson from the Spanish Flu is that the mortality shock was heterogeneous across regions and countries. As discussed in Chapter 3, socioeconomic and climate conditions explain within-country mortality variation in Spain. Similarly, the impact of Covid-19 mortality shock is heterogeneous. This heterogeneity is a consequence of the combination of many factors. The date of the arrival of the pandemic and the reaction of the governments marked the initial mortality differentials. The socioeconomic, age, and racial characteristics of the population correlate with the Covid-19 mortality. Finally, the success of the vaccination process shapes the geographical incidence of Covid-related infections and mortality. We observe that some people do not want to be vaccinated in rich countries even though they have access to them.

Another lesson from the Spanish Flu is that the short-run economic effects were negative and heterogeneous. During the 1918 flu, this heterogeneity was driven mainly by the demand channel, given that physical production was not interrupted during the pandemic. Instead, the process became sophisticated during Covid-19. Bekaert et al. (2020) use real-time survey data for the United States to identify the sources of the fall of GDP during 2020. According to their model, a demand fall explains two-thirds of the GDP decline during the first quarter of 2020. Instead, a supply contraction explains two-thirds of its drop during the second quarter. Therefore, the transmission channel changed during the pandemic.[19]

What forces are behind the changing of the transmission channel during Covid-19 crisis? In the beginning, the population became scared and decided to reduce consumption. It is likely that this consumption contraction was voluntary due to uncertainty, which increased precautionary savings, or forced due to lockdowns and unemployment caused by them. The shock becomes supply-driven when people start to understand the evolution of the disease, and the population income is "guaranteed" by government support or working from home. The global supply chain is the force behind this new phase of the pandemic crisis.[20] Due to the global integration of production, Covid outbreaks, and the subsequent lockdowns, in very distant countries can affect local production and prices (Guan et al., 2020). Instead, during the Spanish flu, this international transmission mechanism was not present because international global markets were already distorted by World War I.[21]

The size of the mortality shock was the main predictor of the country's aggregate economic effects of the 1918 flu. Instead, the countries' income consequences of Covid-19 depend on many factors. The diverse reaction of population and governments (in particular, different lockdown strategies and vaccination speeds), globalization, and unpredictable new variants make the aggregate economic effects of this pandemic hard to forecast.

The International Monetary Fund database (World Economic Outlook, October 2021) shows that the Covid-19 recession was generalized across the globe. Among developed economies, 95% of countries had lower real GDP in 2020 than in 2019. The number for emerging economies with negative growth rates is 81%, but this is an underestimation since data is not already available for all countries. The average fall of GDP was similar to those computed during the Spanish flu: in developed countries was, on average, 6%, and in emerging economies was, on average, 5%. However, these averages masked a substantial dispersion of the economic impact among emerging economies. For example, the GDP in Colombia, Mexico, and Peru fall 7, 8, and 11%, respectively. Instead, real GDP increased 3% in Vietnam and 2% in China. From this dataset, we also obtain suggestive evidence on the relative importance of the pandemic demand shock by looking at inflation rates. Inflation was lower in 92.5% of advanced economies in 2020 compared to the previous year, and average inflation declined from 1.4% in 2019 to 0.4% in 2020. As expected, the demand channel was weaker in the emerging economies since the share of countries with lower inflation was only 53%.

The IMF also predicts an uneven recovery.[22] For example, it expects that in 2022 only 7.5% of developed countries will have a real GDP lower than in 2019. In contrast, it predicts that one out of three emerging economies will have lower real GDP. For 2024 (5 years after the outburst of Covid-19), it expects that still 2.5% of developed economies and 6% of emerging economies will have lower real GDP than in 2019. This recovery is more widespread than after the 2008 financial crisis. The number of advanced countries with lower real GDP in 2013 than in 2008 was 45% among advanced economies and 13% among the emerging ones.

A final lesson from the Spanish Flu is that inequality increased (Basco et al., 2021). Although it is too early to draw definitive conclusions, the preliminary evidence points in the same direction for the Covid-19 pandemic. The IMF reports that the decline in employment between the last quarter of 2019 and the first quarter of 2021 was more intense among young (15–24 years) and low-skill workers. This pattern is common to both advanced and developing economies. Credit Suisse (2021) shows that global wealth inequality increased in 2020 by a substantial amount. This increase in inequality was generalized and robust to different measures of inequality (share of the top 10%, the top 1%, and the Gini coefficient).

The United States is an example of this increase in inequality. In this country, the wealth share of the top 1% has increased from 35 to 35.3% during 2021. The main reason for this pattern is that wealthier people own a disproportionate share of capital and, thus, they benefit relatively more from a rise in capital returns (e.g., stock prices and house prices).[23] Standard and Poor's 500, one of the most followed equity indices, has increased roughly 26%[24] and average housing prices about 19% during 2021.[25] In comparison, the average hourly earnings have grown about 10% during the same period.[26] A similar picture would likely emerge for other advanced economies (Credit Suisse, 2021). How to tackle the potential persistent redistributive effects of pandemics is a critical policy question, but it is outside the scope of this book.

To summarize, according to the evidence collected in this book, pre-industrial pandemics cannot be employed to predict the economic consequences of Covid-19. Instead, the Spanish flu offers many insights to understand the current Covid-19 pandemic. Above all, the impact of the 1918 flu pandemic was heterogeneous. Mortality differed across countries, regions, and social classes. Workers experienced more economic damage and mortality than capital owners and the pandemic increased socioeconomic inequality. Income losses were also unevenly distributed across countries and regions. We can conclude that there were winners and losers everywhere. Moreover, the world did not become more equal and grew because of the pandemic. Therefore, the optimistic view on pandemics has little empirical justification. In the modern world, pandemics are not "Great Levelers".

Notes

1. The real money balances are the ratio between money supply and prices.
2. All these effects depend on the organizational structure of the economy during the pandemic. Specifically, aggregate demand shifts are contingent on pandemic information, workers bargaining power, country development levels, personal savings, and the kind of job.
3. Bloom (2014) discusses the role of uncertainty in modern economies.
4. This view is confirmed indirectly by Koudijs and Voth (2016). Using a speculative financial event in Amsterdam (1772), these authors document that personal experiences (fear to lose) can affect future risk behaviour. However, they also pointed out that not-at-risk investors did not change their behaviour, even though they were also aware of the evolution of the financial markets. Thus, it seems likely that future generations can forget about financial and economic crises.
5. Point 0 in Panel B of Fig. 6.1 represents the long-run equilibrium.
6. Weil (2014) reviews the existing literature and evidence on contemporary economies. He finds that per capita GDP and mortality (as other health indicators) are strongly correlated. The historical evolution of cross-country mortality differences has largely paralleled per capita income differences. Nevertheless, in the last half-century, the convergence of mortality has been much faster than the convergence of income. The causal channel between income and mortality operates in both directions, but its magnitude is limited. The author attributes this result to the fact that other factors, like institutions and human capital accumulation, raise income and improve mortality simultaneously.
7. North (1981) was one of the first economists to relate institutions to economic development. Literature pointed out that rich countries tend to have "good institutions". There is no agreement about the definition of "good institutions", the Worldwide Governance Indicators of the World Bank report on six dimensions: voice and accountability, political stability, government effectiveness, regulatory quality, rule-of-law, and control of corruption. https://info.worldbank.org/governance/wgi/.
8. Others have interpreted the Black Death using a "Smithian" framework. According to this view, even during the pre-industrial period, there was a positive relationship, not negative, between population density and economic growth. The reason was that the growing population led to increasing division of labour, specialization, and commercialization. See, among others, Boserup, (1965), Grantham, (1999), Hatcher and Bailey (2001), and Broadberry et al., (2015).
9. There is an ample literature on this. See, for example, De Pleijt and Van Zanden (2016).

10. There are many contributions on this topic. For a recent summary, for example, Court (2020).
11. For a review of this debate, see Jedwab et al. (2021).
12. See, among others, the surveys of Arthi and Parman (2021), Boianovsky and Erreygers (2021), Burdekin (2020), Callegari and Feder (2021), and Cohen-Kristiansen and Pinheiro (2020).
13. Note that, in our theoretical model, we considered aggregate output. If GDP per capita declined, it means that GDP (aggregate output) declined even more.
14. Correia et al. (2020) uses variation in the degree and intensity of nonpharmaceutical interventions (lockdown) and found that cities that intervened earlier and more aggressively did not perform worse and, if anything, grew faster after the epidemic.
15. There are no parallel pre-trends for urban GDP. This exacerbates the urban GDP coefficient. However, given that GDP is falling, and rural GDP is not changing, it seems clear that urban GDP is responsible for this overall GDP fall.
16. A suggestive hypothesis that requires further research is that the 1918 Flu led to structural change in Spain, shifting production from high to low mortality regions. The evidence of Chapter 5 on capital reallocation is consistent with this hypothesis.
17. We cannot perform a differences-in-differences exercise, which would have granted more credibility to this result because the pre-shock data violate the required assumptions (parallel trends).
18. We refer the reader to Chapter 5 for an in-depth discussion of their findings.
19. This result may be idiosyncratic because the fiscal and monetary policies in the United States were exceptional (especially the stimulus and relief packages announced in March 2020) compared to other developed economies. See a review of the different stimulus packages at International Monetary Fund (2022).
20. The formation of global supply chains began in the early 1990s. It is related to the IT revolution (see, for example, Basco and Mestieri, 2019). This fragmentation of production means that firms have input providers from all over the world. For example, firm A located in country X uses an input produced in firm B in country Y. If there is a lockdown in country Y (or firm B did not keep inventory or cannot supply the demanded inputs), it will affect the cost (and/or quantity) of the inputs and, thus, the production in country X.
21. A review of this de-globalization process is available at Eloranta and Harrison (2010).
22. These predictions are those available by October 2021. The next set of predictions will be available by April 2022 after the writing of this book.

23. According to US Federal Reserve data, the wealthiest 10% owned, in the second quarter of 2021, the 89%of US corporate equities and mutual funds and the top 1% owned the 54%. The corresponding numbers for real estate assets are 45 and 14%. It implies that an increment in the stock market indices or housing prices will increase wealth inequality. https://www.federalreserve.gov/releases/z1/dataviz/dfa/distribute/chart/#quarter:127;series:Corporate%20equities%20and%20mutual%20fund%20shares;demographic:networth;population:all;units:shares.
24. The data on S & P 500 is available at: https://www.spglobal.com/spdji/en/indices/equity/sp-500/#overview.
25. The data is drawn from the Case-Shiller house price index. https://www.spglobal.com/spdji/en/indices/indicators/sp-corelogic-case-shiller-us-national-home-price-nsa-index/#overview.
26. https://fred.stlouisfed.org/series/CES0500000003#0.

References

Acemoglu, D. (2002). Directed technical change. *Review of Economic Studies*, 69(4), 781–809.

Alfani, G., & Murphy, T. (2017). Plague and lethal epidemics in the pre-industrial world. *Journal of Economic History*, 77(1), 314–343.

Almond, D. (2006). Is the 1918 influenza pandemic over? Long-term effects of in utero influenza exposure in the post-1940 U.S. population. *Journal of Political Economy*, 114(4), 672–712.

Álvarez Nogal, C., Prados de la Escosura, L., & Santiago Caballero, C. (2021). *Economic effects of the Black Death: Spain in European perspective* (Instituto Figuerola Working Papers in Economic History, 2020-06).

Arthi, V., & Parman, J. (2021). Disease, downturns, and wellbeing: Economic history and the long-run impacts of COVID-19. *Explorations in Economic History*, 79, 101381.

Barro, R., Ursúa, J., & Weng, J. (2020). *The coronavirus and the great influenza pandemic. Lessons from the "Spanish Flu" for the coronavirus's potential effects on mortality and economic activity* (NBER Working Papers 26866).

Basco, S., & Mestieri, M. (2019). The world income distribution: The effects of international unbundling of production. *Journal of Economic Growth*, 24, 189–221.

Basco, S., Domènech, J., & Rosés, J. R. (2021). The redistributive effects of pandemics: Evidence from the Spanish Flu. *World Development*, 141, 105389.

Bekaert, G., Engstrom, E., & Ermolov, A. (2020). *Aggregate demand and aggregate supply effects of COVID-19: A real-time analysis* (Board of Governors of the Federal Reserve System, Finance and Economics Discussion Series, 2020-049).

Benmelech, E., & Frydman, C. (2020). The 1918 influenza did not kill the US economy, *Vox CEPR Policy Portal*.
Bloom, N. (2014). Fluctuations in uncertainty. *Journal of Economic Perspectives*, 28(2), 153–176.
Boianovsky, M., & Erreygers, G. (2021). How economists ignored the Spanish Flu pandemic in 1918–1920. *Erasmus Journal for Philosophy and Economics*, 14(1), 89–109.
Boserup, E. (1965). *The conditions of agricultural growth: The economics of Agrarian change under population pressure*. Aldine.
Broadberry, S. N. (2021). *Accounting for the great divergence: Recent findings from historical national accounting* (CEPR Discussion Papers, 15936).
Broadberry, S. N., Campbell, B., Klein, A., Overton, M., & van Leeuwen, B. (2015). *British economic growth, 1270–1870*. Cambridge University Press.
Burdekin, R. C. (2020). Economic and financial effects of the 1918–1919 Spanish Flu pandemic. *Journal of Infectious Diseases and Therapy*, 8, 1000439.
Callegari, B., & Feder, C. (2021). The long-term economic effects of pandemics: Toward an evolutionary approach. *Industrial and Corporate Change*, forthcoming.
Carillo, M. F., & Jappelli, T. (2022). Pandemics and regional economic growth: Evidence from the Great Influenza in Italy. *European Review of Economic History*, 26(1), 78–106.
Cohen-Kristiansen, R., & Pinheiro, R. (2020). *The 1918 flu and COVID-19 pandemics: Different patients, different economy* (Economic Commentary 2020-13).
Correia, S., Luck, S., & Verner, E. (2020). *Fight the pandemic, save the economy: Lessons from the 1918 flu* (Federal Reserve Bank of New York Working Papers, 5).
Court, V. (2020). A reassessment of the Great Divergence debate: Towards a reconciliation of apparently distinct determinants. *European Review of Economic History*, 24(4), 633–674.
Credit Suisse. (2021). *Global Wealth Report. Effects of COVID on household wealth*. https://www.credit-suisse.com/about-us-news/en/articles/news-and-expertise/global-wealth-report-2021-effects-of-covid-on-household-wealth-in-2020-202106.html
Dahl, C. M., Hansen, C. W., & Jensen, P. S. (2020). The 1918 epidemic and a V-shaped recession: Evidence from municipal income data. *Covid Economics*, 6: 137–162.
De Pleijt, A. M., & Van Zanden, J. L. (2016). Accounting for the "Little Divergence": What drove economic growth in pre-industrial Europe, 1300–1800? *European Review of Economic History*, 20(4), 387–409.
De Santis, R. A., & Van der Veken, W. (2020). *Macroeconomic risks across the globe due to the Spanish Flu* (ECB Working Paper Series, No. 2466).

Eloranta, J., & Harrison, M. (2010). War and disintegration, 1914–1950. *The Cambridge Economic History of Modern Europe, 2*, 133–156.

Gallardo-, D., & Zwart, P. (2021). A bitter epidemic: The impact of the 1918 influenza on sugar production in Java. *Economics and Human Biology, 42*, 101011.

Grantham, G. W. (1999). Contra Ricardo: On the macroeconomics of pre-industrial economies. *European Review of Economic History, 3*(2), 199–232.

Guan, D., Wang, D., Hallegatte, S., Davis, S., Huo, J., Li, S., Bai, Y., Lei, T., Xue, Q., Coffman, D., Cheng, D., Chen, P., Liang, X., Xu, B., Lu, X., Wang, S., Hubacek, K., & Gong, P. (2020). Global supply-chain effects of COVID-19 control measures. *Nature Human Behaviour, 4*(6), 577–587.

Guimbeau, A., Menon, N., & Musacchio, A. (2021). Short and medium-run health and literacy impacts of the 1918 Spanish Flu pandemic in Brazil. *Economic History Review*, forthcoming.

Harper, K. (2016). People, plagues, and prices in the Roman world: The evidence from Egypt. *Journal of Economic History, 76*(3), 803–839.

Hatcher, J., & Bailey, M. (2001). *Modelling the middle ages*. Oxford University Press.

Helgertz, J., & Bengtsson, T. (2019). The long-lasting influenza: The impact of fetal stress during the 1918 influenza pandemic on socioeconomic attainment and health in Sweden, 1968–2012. *Demography, 56*(4), 1389–1425.

Hong, S. C., & Yun, Y. (2017). Fetal exposure to the 1918 influenza pandemic in colonial Korea and human capital development. *Seoul Journal of Economics, 30*(4), 353–383.

International Monetary Fund. (2022). *Policy Responses to COVID-19*. https://www.imf.org/en/Topics/imf-and-covid19/Policy-Responses-to-COVID-19

Jedwab, R., Johnson, N., & Koyama, M. (2021). The economic impact of the Black Death. *Journal of Economic Literature*, forthcoming.

Karlsson, M., Nilsson, T., & Pichler, S. (2014). The impact of the 1918 Spanish flu epidemic on economic performance in Sweden: An investigation into the consequences of an extraordinary mortality shock. *Journal of Health Economics, 36*(1), 1–19.

Koudijs, P., & Voth, H.-J. (2016). Leverage and beliefs: Personal experience and risk taking in margin lending. *American Economic Review, 106*, 3367–3400.

North, D. C. (1981). *Structure and change in economic history*. W. W. Norton.

Noy, I., Okubo, T., & Strobl, E. (2020). *The Japanese textile sector and the influenza pandemic of 1918–1920* (CESifo Working Papers, 8651).

Pamuk, Ş. (2007). The Black Death and the origins of the 'Great Divergence' across Europe, 1300–1600. *European Review of Economic History, 11*(3): 289–317.

Parman, J. (2015). Childhood health and sibling outcomes: Nurture Reinforcing nature during the 1918 influenza pandemic. *Explorations in Economic History, 58*(91), 22–43.

Prados de la Escosura, L. (2017). *Spanish economic growth, 1850–2015*. Palgrave Macmillan.

Prados, L., & Rosés, J. R. (2009). The sources of long-run growth in Spain, 1850–2000. *Journal of Economic History, 69*(4), 1063–1091.

Velde, F. R. (2020). *What happened to the US economy during the 1918 influenza pandemic? A view through high-frequency data* (Federal Reserve Bank of Chicago Working Papers, 2020-11).

Voigtländer, N., & Voth, H.-J. (2013). The three horsemen of riches: Plague, war, and urbanization in early modern Europe. *Review of Economic Studies, 80*(2), 774–811.

Weil, D. N. (2014). Health and Economic Growth. *Handbook of Economic Growth, 2*(3), 623–682.

World Economic Outlook. (2021, October). *International Monetary Fund*. Imf Publications. https://www.imf.org/en/Publications/WEO/weo-database/2021/October

REFERENCES

Abramovitz, M. (1956). Resource and output trends in the United States since 1870. *American Economic Review, 46*(1), 5–23.

Acemoglu, D. (2002). Directed technical change. *Review of Economic Studies, 69*(4), 781–809.

Acemoglu, D., & Johnson, S. (2007). Disease and development: The effect of life expectancy on economic growth. *Journal of Political Economy, 115*(6), 925–985.

Acemoglu, D., & Robinson, J. (2013). *Why national fail: The origins of power, prosperity, and poverty*. Crown Business.

Acuña-Soto, R., Stahle, D. W., Cleaveland, M. K., & Therrell, M. D. (2002). Megadrought and megadeath in 16th century Mexico. *Emerging Infectious Diseases, 8*(4), 360–362.

Alfani, G. (2015). Economic inequality in Northwestern Italy: A long-term view (fourteenth to eighteenth centuries). *Journal of Economic History, 75*(4), 1058–1096.

Alfani, G. (2022). Epidemics, inequality, and poverty in preindustrial and early industrial times. *Journal of Economic Literature, 60*(1), 3–40.

Alfani, G., & Murphy, T. (2017). Plague and lethal epidemics in the pre-industrial world. *Journal of Economic History, 77*(1), 314–343.

Allen, R. C. (2001). The great divergence in European wages and prices in Europe from the Middle Ages to the First World War. *Explorations in Economic History, 38*(4), 411–447.

Allen, R. C. (2011). *Global economic history*. Oxford University Press.

Almond, D. (2006). Is the 1918 influenza pandemic over? Long-term effects of in utero influenza exposure in the post-1940 U.S. population. *Journal of Political Economy, 114*(4), 672–712.

Alonso, W. J., Viboud, C., Simonsen, L., Hirano, E. W., Daufenbach, L. Z., & Miller, M. A. (2007). Seasonality of influenza in Brazil: A traveling wave from the Amazon to the subtropics. *American Journal of Epidemiology, 165*(12), 1434–1442.

Álvarez Nogal, C., Prados de la Escosura, L., & Santiago Caballero, C. (2021). *Economic effects of the Black Death: Spain in European perspective* (Instituto Figuerola Working Papers in Economic History, 2020-06).

Anderson, R. M., & May, R. M. (1992). *Infectious diseases of humans: Dynamics and control* (28th ed.). Oxford University Press.

Arango, J. (1980). La teoría de la transición demográfica y la experiencia histórica. *Reis, 10*(1), 169–198.

Arthi, V., & Parman, J. (2021). Disease, downturns, and wellbeing: Economic history and the long-run impacts of COVID-19. *Explorations in Economic History, 79*, 101381.

Azizi, M. H., Raees, G. H., & Azizi, F. (2010). A history of the 1918 Spanish influenza pandemic and its impact on Iran. *Archives of Iranian Medicine, 13*(3), 262–265.

Bambra, C., Riordan, R., Ford, J., & Matthews, F. (2020). The COVID-19 pandemic and health inequalities. *Journal of Epidemiol Community Health, 74*(11), 964–968.

Barry, J. M. (2004). *The great influenza: The story of the deadliest pandemic in history*. Penguin.

Barry, J. M., Viboud, C., & Simonsen, L. (2008). Cross-protection between successive waves of the 1918–1919 influenza pandemic: Epidemiological evidence from US Army camps and from Britain. *Journal of Infectious Diseases, 198*(10), 1427e34.

Barro, R., Ursúa, J., & Weng, J. (2020). *The coronavirus and the great influenza pandemic. Lessons from the "Spanish Flu" for the coronavirus's potential effects on mortality and economic activity* (NBER Working Papers 26866).

Basco, S. (2018). *Housing bubbles*. Palgrave Macmillan.

Basco, S., Domènech, J., & Rosés, J. R. (2021a). The redistributive effects of pandemics: Evidence from the Spanish Flu. *World Development, 141*, 105389.

Basco, S., Domènech, J., & Rosés, J. R. (2021b). *Unequal Mortality during the Spanish Flu* (CEPR Discussion Papers, 15783).

Basco, S., Domènech, J., & Rosés, J. R. (2021c). *Capital market, mortgage credit and pandemics: Evidence from the Spanish Flu*. mimeo.

Basco, S., & Mestieri, M. (2019). The world income distribution: The effects of international unbundling of production. *Journal of Economic Growth, 24*, 189–221.

Baud, D., Qi, X., Nielsen-Saines, K., Musso, D., Pomar, L., & Favre, G. (2020). Real estimates of mortality following COVID-19 infection. *Lancet Infectious Diseases, 20*(7), 773.

Beaney, T., Clarke, J. C., Jain, V., Golestaneh, A. K., Lyons, G., Salman, D., & Majeed, A. (2020). Excess mortality: The gold standard in measuring the impact of COVID-19 worldwide? *Journal of the Royal Society of Medicine, 113*(9), 329–334.

Bekaert, G., Engstrom, E., & Ermolov, A. (2020). *Aggregate demand and aggregate supply effects of COVID-19: A real-time analysis* (Board of Governors of the Federal Reserve System, Finance and Economics Discussion Series, 2020-049).

Bengtsson, T., Dribe, M., & Eriksson, B. (2018). Social class and excess mortality in Sweden during the 1918 influenza pandemic. *American Journal of Epidemiology, 187*(12), 2568–2576.

Benmelech, E., & Frydman, C. (2020). The 1918 influenza did not kill the US economy, *Vox CEPR Policy Portal*.

Berkes, E., Deschenes, O., Gaetani, R., Lin, J., & Severen, C. (2020). *Lockdowns and innovation: Evidence from the 1918 flu pandemic* (NBER Working Papers, w28152).

Bloom-Feshbach, K., Alonso, W. J., Charu, V., Tamerius, J., Simonsen, L., Miller, M. A., & Viboud, C. (2013). Latitudinal variations in seasonal activity of influenza and respiratory syncytial virus (RSV): A global comparative review. *PLoS ONE, 8*(2), e54445.

Bloom, N. (2014). Fluctuations in uncertainty. *Journal of Economic Perspectives, 28*(2), 153–176.

Boianovsky, M., & Erreygers, G. (2021). How economists ignored the Spanish Flu pandemic in 1918–1920. *Erasmus Journal for Philosophy and Economics, 14*(1), 89–109.

Bolt, J., & van Zanden, J. L. (2020). *Maddison style estimates of the evolution of the world economy. A new 2020 update* (Maddison-Project Working Paper WP-15).

Bootsma, M. C. J., & Ferguson, N. M. (2007). Public health interventions and epidemic intensity during the 1918 influenza pandemic. *Proceedings of the National Academy of Sciences, 104*(18), 7588–7593.

Boserup, E. (1965). *The conditions of agricultural growth: The economics of Agrarian change under population pressure*. Aldine.

Bowman, A. (2014). *Epidemics and mortality in early modern Japan*. Princeton University Press.

Brainerd, E., & Siegler, M. (2003). *The economic effects of the 1918 influenza pandemic* (CEPR Discussion Papers, 3791).

Bramanti, B., Dean, K. R., Walløe, L., & Stenseth, N. C. (2019). The third plague pandemic in Europe. *Proceedings of the Royal Society B: Biological Sciences, 286*(1901), 20182429.

Broadberry, S. N. (2021). *Accounting for the great divergence: Recent findings from historical national accounting* (CEPR Discussion Papers, 15936).

Broadberry, S. N., Campbell, B., Klein, A., Overton, M., & van Leeuwen, B. (2015). *British economic growth, 1270–1870*. Cambridge University Press.

Broadberry, S. N., & Harrison, M. (Eds.). (2005). *The economics of World War I*. Cambridge University Press.

Broadberry, S. N., & Harrison, M. (Eds.). (2018). *The economics of the Great War: A centennial perspective*. CEPR Press.

Brown, C., & Ravallion, M. (2020). *Inequality and the coronavirus: Socio-economic covariates of behavioral responses and viral outcomes across us counties* (NBER Working Papers, w27549).

Brundage, J. F., & Shanks, G. D. (2008). Deaths from bacterial pneumonia during 1918–19 influenza pandemic. *Emerging Infectious Diseases, 14*(8), 1193.

Burdekin, R. C. (2020). Economic and financial effects of the 1918–1919 Spanish flu pandemic. *Journal of Infectious Diseases and Therapy, 8*, 1000439.

Byerly, C. R. (2010). The US military and the influenza pandemic of 1918–1919. *Public Health Reports, 125*(Supp. 3), 81–91.

Cain, L., & Hong, S. C. (2009). Survival in 19th century cities: The larger the city, the smaller your chances. *Explorations in Economic History, 46*(4), 450–463.

Callegari, B., & Feder, C. (2021). The long-term economic effects of pandemics: Toward an evolutionary approach. *Industrial and Corporate Change*, forthcoming.

Callegari, B., & Feder, C. (2022). A literature review of pandemics and development: The long-term perspective. *Economics of Disasters and Climate Change, 6*, 183–212.

Caramelo, F., Ferreira, N., & Oliveiros, B. (2020). Estimation of risk factors for COVID-19 mortality-preliminary results. *MedRxiv*.

Carillo, M. F., & Jappelli, T. (2022). Pandemics and regional economic growth: Evidence from the Great Influenza in Italy. *European Review of Economic History, 26*(1), 78–106.

Carmona, J., Lampe, M., & Rosés, J. (2017). Housing affordability during the urban transition in Spain. *The Economic History Review, 70*(2), 632–658.

Carmona, J., Lampe, M., & Rosés, J. R. (2014). Spanish housing markets, 1904–1934: New evidence. *Revista de Historia Económica/Journal of Iberian and Latin American Economic History, 32*(1), 119–150.

Chandra, S. (2013). Deaths associated with influenza pandemic of 1918–19 Japan. *Emerging Infectious Diseases, 19*(4), 616–622.

Chandra, S. (2014). Mortality from the influenza pandemic of 1918–1919 in Indonesia. *Population Studies, 67*(2), 185–193.
Chandra, S., & Kassens-Noor, E. (2014). The evolution of the pandemic influenza: Evidence from India, 1918–1919. *BMC Infectious Diseases, 14*, 510.
Chandra, S., Kuljanin, G., & Way, J. (2012). Mortality from the pandemic of 1918–1919: The case of India. *Demography, 49*(3), 857–865.
Chen, J. T., & Krieger, N. (2021). Revealing the unequal burden of COVID-19 by income, race/ethnicity, and household crowding: US county versus zip code analyses. *Journal of Public Health Management and Practice, 27*(1), S43–S56.
Cheshire, P., Hilber, C., & Schöni, O. (2021). *The pandemic and the housing market: A British story* (CEP Covid-19 Papers, 020).
Chowell, G., Bettencourt, L. M., Johnson, N., Alonso, W. J., & Viboud, C. (2008). The 1918–1919 influenza pandemic in England and Wales: Spatial patterns in transmissibility and mortality impact. *Proceedings of the Royal Society B: Biological Sciences, 275*(1634), 501–509.
Chowell, G., Erkoreka, A., Viboud, C., & Echeverri-Dávila, B. (2014). Spatial-temporal excess mortality patterns of the 1918–1919 influenza pandemic in Spain. *BMC Infectious Diseases, 14*, 371.
Chowell, G., Simonsen, L., Flores, J., Miller, M. A., & Viboud, C. (2014). Death patterns during the 1918 influenza pandemic in Chile. *Emerging Infectious Diseases, 20*(11), 1803–1811.
Christakos, G., Olea, R., Serre, M., Yu, H., & Wang, L. (2005). *Interdisciplinary public health reasoning and epidemic modelling: The case of Black Death*. Springer.
Cilek, L., Chowell, G., & Ramiro Fariñas, D. (2018). Age-specific excess mortality patterns during the 1918–1920 influenza pandemic in Madrid Spain. *American Journal of Epidemiology, 187*(12), 2511–2523.
Cirillo, P., & Taleb, N. N. (2020). Tail risk of contagious diseases. *Nature Physics, 16*, 606–613.
Clark, G. (2008). *A farewell to Alms*. Princeton University Press.
Clay, K., Lewis, J., & Severnini, E. (2018). Pollution, infectious disease, and mortality: Evidence from the 1918 Spanish influenza pandemic. *Journal of Economic History, 78*(4), 1179–1209.
Clay, K., Lewis, J., & Severnini, E. (2019). What explains cross-city variation in mortality during the 1918 influenza pandemic? Evidence from 438 US cities. *Economics and Human Biology, 35*, 42–50.
Cohen-Kristiansen, R., & Pinheiro, R. (2020). *The 1918 flu and COVID-19 pandemics: Different patients, different economy* (Economic Commentary 2020-13).

Collcutt, M. (1987). Review "population, disease, and land in early Japan, 645–900 William Wayne Farris." *Harvard Journal of Asiatic Studies, 47*(1), 299–310.

Collier, R. (1996). *The plague of the Spanish Lady*. Allison and Busby.

Colvin, C. L., & McLaughlin, E. (2021). Death, demography and the denominator: Age-adjusted influenza-18 mortality in Ireland. *Economics and Human Biology, 41*, 100984.

Correia, S., Luck, S., & Verner, E. (2020). *Fight the pandemic, save the economy: Lessons from the 1918 flu* (Federal Reserve Bank of New York Working Papers, 5).

Court, V. (2020). A reassessment of the Great Divergence debate: Towards a reconciliation of apparently distinct determinants. *European Review of Economic History, 24*(4), 633–674.

Credit Suisse. (2021). *Global Wealth Report. Effects of COVID on household wealth.* https://www.credit-suisse.com/about-us-news/en/articles/news-and-expertise/global-wealth-report-2021-effects-of-covid-on-household-wealth-in-2020-202106.html

Crosby, A. W. (2003). *Americ"s forgotten pandemic: The influenza of 1918*. Cambridge University Press.

Dahl, C. M., Hansen, C. W., & Jensen, P. S. (2020). The 1918 epidemic and a V-shaped recession: Evidence from municipal income data. *Covid Economics, 6:* 137–162.

Davis, K. (1951). *The population of India and Pakistan*. Princeton University Press.

Deaton, A. (2013). *The great escape*. Princeton University Press.

Demombynes, G. (2020). *COVID-19 age-mortality curves are flatter in developing countries* (World Bank Policy Research Working Paper, 9313).

De Pleijt, A. M., & Van Zanden, J. L. (2016). Accounting for the "Little Divergence": What drove economic growth in pre-industrial Europe, 1300–1800? *European Review of Economic History, 20*(4), 387–409.

De Santis, R. A., & Van der Veken, W. (2020). *Macroeconomic risks across the globe due to the Spanish Flu* (ECB Working Paper Series, No. 2466).

D'Lima, W., Lopez, L. A., & Pradhan, A. (2021). COVID-19 and housing market effects: Evidence from us shutdown orders. *Real Estate Economics*, forthcoming.

Echeverrri, B. (1985). *La gripe Española. La pandemia de 1918–1919*. Centro de Investigaciones Sociológicas (CIS).

Elgar, F. J., Stefaniak, A., & Wohl, M. J. (2020). The trouble with trust: Time-series analysis of social capital, income inequality, and COVID-19 deaths in 84 countries. *Social Science and Medicine, 263*, 113365.

Eloranta, J., & Harrison, M. (2010). War and disintegration, 1914–1950. *The Cambridge Economic History of Modern Europe, 2*, 133–156.

Evans, R. (2006). *Death in Hamburg: Society and politics in the Cholera years 1830–1910*. Penguin.
Farris, W. W. (2020). *Population, disease, and land in early Japan, 645-900*. Brill.
Feigenbaum, J., Muller, C., & Wrigley-Field, E. (2019). Regional and racial inequality in infectious disease mortality in U.S. cities, 1900–1948. *Demography, 56*, 1371–1388.
Fortson, J. G. (2011). Mortality risk and human capital investment: The impact of HIV/AIDS in Sub-Saharan Africa. *Review of Economics and Statistics, 93*(1), 1–15.
Friedman, M., & Schwartz, A. (1963). *A monetary history of the United States (1867–1960)*. Princeton University Press.
Gagnon, A., Miller, M. S., Hallman, S. A., Bourbeau, R., Herring, D. A., Earn, D. J., & Madrenas, J. (2013). Age-specific mortality during the 1918 influenza pandemic: Unravelling the mystery of high young adult mortality. *PLoS ONE, 8*(8), e69586.
Gallardo-Albarrán, D., & Zwart, P. (2021). A bitter epidemic: The impact of the 1918 influenza on sugar production in Java. *Economics and Human Biology, 42*, 101011.
Gallent, N., & Madeddu, M. (2021). Covid-19 and London's decentralising housing market—What are the planning implications? *Planning Practice and Research, 36*(5), 567–577.
Galletta, S., & Giommoni, T. (2020). *The effect of the 1918 influenza pandemic on income inequality: Evidence from Italy* (COVID Economics: Vetted and Real-time Papers 33).
Galor, O. (2011). *Unified growth theory*. Princeton University Press.
García Delgado, J. L., Roldán, S., & Muñoz, J. (1973). *La Formación de la Sociedad Capitalista en España (1914–1920)*. CECA.
García Gómez, J. J. (2016). Urban penalty en España: el caso de Alcoy (1857–1930). *Revista de Historia Industrial, 25*(63): 49–78.
Garrett, T. A. (2009). War and pestilence as labor market shocks: US manufacturing wage growth 1914–1919. *Economic Inquiry, 47*(4), 711–725.
Gil Ibáñez, S. (1978). Un intento de homogeneización de las clasificaciones profesionales en España (1860–1930). *Revista Internacional de Sociología, 25*, 7–40.
Goerlich Gisbert, F. J. (2012). Datos climáticos históricos para las regiones españolas. CRU TS 2.1. *Investigaciones de Historia Económica, 8*(1), 29–40.
Grantham, G. W. (1999). Contra Ricardo: On the macroeconomics of pre-industrial economies. *European Review of Economic History, 3*(2), 199–232.
Grantz, K. H., Rane, M. S., Salje, H., Glass, G. E., Schachterle, S. E., & Cummings, D. A. (2016). Disparities in influenza mortality and transmission related to sociodemographic factors within Chicago in the pandemic of 1918. *Proceedings of the National Academy of Sciences, 113*(48), 13839–13844.

Greif, A. (2006). *Institutions and the path to the modern economy*. Cambridge University Press.
Guan, D., Wang, D., Hallegatte, S., Davis, S., Huo, J., Li, S., Bai, Y., Lei, T., Xue, Q., Coffman, D., Cheng, D., Chen, P., Liang, X., Xu, B., Lu, X., Wang, S., Hubacek, K., & Gong, P. (2020). Global supply-chain effects of COVID-19 control measures. *Nature Human Behaviour*, 4(6), 577–587.
Guimbeau, A., Menon, N., & Musacchio, A. (2021). Short and medium-run health and literacy impacts of the 1918 Spanish Flu pandemic in Brazil. *Economic History Review*, forthcoming.
Haines, M. R. (2001). The urban mortality transition in the United States, 1800–1940. *Annales de démographie historique*, 1, 33–64.
Harper, K. (2016). People, plagues, and prices in the Roman world: The evidence from Egypt. *Journal of Economic History*, 76(3), 803–839.
Hatcher, J., & Bailey, M. (2001). *Modelling the middle ages*. Oxford University Press.
Hatchett, R. J., Mecher, C. E., & Lipsitch, M. (2007). Public health interventions and epidemic intensity during the 1918 influenza pandemic. *Proceedings of the National Academy of Sciences*, 104(18), 7582–7587.
Helgertz, J., & Bengtsson, T. (2019). The long-lasting influenza: The impact of fetal stress during the 1918 influenza pandemic on socioeconomic attainment and health in Sweden, 1968–2012. *Demography*, 56(4), 1389–1425.
Herrera-Diestra, J. L., & Meyers, L. A. (2019). Local risk perception enhances epidemic control. *PLoS ONE*, 14(12), e0225576.
Herring, D. A., & Korol, E. (2012). The north-south divide: Social inequality and mortality from the 1918 influenza pandemic in Hamilton, Ontario. In M. Fahrni & E. W. Jones (Eds.), *Epidemic encounters: Influenza, society, and culture in Canada* (pp. 97–112). University of Toronto Press.
Hong, S. C., & Yun, Y. (2017). Fetal exposure to the 1918 influenza pandemic in colonial Korea and human capital development. *Seoul Journal of Economics*, 30(4), 353–383.
International Monetary Fund. (2022). *Policy Responses to COVID-19*. https://www.imf.org/en/Topics/imf-and-covid19/Policy-Responses-to-COVID-19
Jay, J., Bor, J., Nsoesie, E. O., Lipson, S. K., Jones, D. K., Galea, S., & Raifman, J. (2020). Neighbourhood income and physical distancing during the COVID-19 pandemic in the United States. *Nature Human Behaviour*, 4(12), 1294–1302.
Jedwab, R., Johnson, N., & Koyama, M. (2021). The economic impact of the Black Death. *Journal of Economic Literature*, forthcoming.
Johnson, N., & Mueller, J. (2002). Updating the accounts: Global mortality of the 1918–1920 "Spanish" influenza pandemic. *Bulletin of the History of Medicine*, 76, 105–115.

Jones, C. I., & Klenow, P. J. (2016). Beyond GDP? Welfare across countries and time. *American Economic Review, 106*(9), 2426–2457.
Jordà, Ò., Knoll, K., Kuvshinov, D., Schularick, M., & Taylor, A. M. (2019). The rate of return on everything, 1870–2015. *Quarterly Journal of Economics, 134*, 1225–1298.
Jordà, Ò., Schularick, M., & Taylor, A. M. (2013). When credit bites back. *Journal of Money, Credit and Banking, 45*, 3–28.
Jordà, Ò., Singh, S. R., & Taylor, A. M. (2021). Longer-run economic consequences of pandemics. *Review of Economics and Statistics*, forthcoming.
Kalemli-Ozcan, S., & Turan, B. (2011). HIV and fertility revisited. *Journal of Development Economics, 96*(1), 61–65.
Karlsson, M., Nilsson, T., & Pichler, S. (2014). The impact of the 1918 Spanish flu epidemic on economic performance in Sweden: An investigation into the consequences of an extraordinary mortality shock. *Journal of Health Economics, 36*(1), 1–19.
Keeling, A. W. (2020). The 1918 influenza pandemic: Lessons from the past for a global community. *Health Emergency and Disaster Nursing, 7*(1), 27–28.
Keynes, J. M. (1920). *The economic consequences of peace*. Macmillan.
Klein, S. L., Hodgson, A., & Robinson, D. P. (2012). Mechanisms of sex disparities in influenza pathogenesis. *Journal of Leukocyte Biology, 92*(1), 67–73.
Kolata, G. (1999). *Flu: The story of the great influenza pandemic of 1918 and the search for the virus that caused it*. Simon and Schuster.
Koudijs, P., & Voth, H.-J. (2016). Leverage and beliefs: Personal experience and risk taking in margin lending. *American Economic Review, 106*, 3367–3400.
Kwok, K. O., Li, K. K., Chan, H. H. H., Yi, Y. Y., Tang, A., Wei, W. I., & Wong, S. Y. S. (2020). Community responses during early phase of COVID-19 epidemic, Hong Kong. *Emerging Infectious Diseases, 26*(7), 1575.
Lacomba, J. A., Ruiz, G., de la Macorra, L., & Ruiz, A. (1990). *Una historia del Banco Hipotecario de España*. Alianza Editorial.
Lee, R. (2003). The demographic transition: Three centuries of fundamental change. *Journal of Economic Perspectives, 17*(4), 167–190.
Lee, J., & Huang, Y. (2022). Covid-19 impact on US housing markets: Evidence from spatial regression models. *Spatial Economic Analysis*, forthcoming.
Le Moglie, M., Gandolfi, F., Alfani, G., & Aassve, A. (2020). *Epidemics and trust: The case of the Spanish Flu* (IGIER Working Papers, 661).
Lilley, A., Lilley, M., & Rinaldi, G. (2020). *Public health interventions and economic growth: Revisiting the Spanish flu evidence*. SSRN 3590008.
Luk, L., Gross, P., & Thompson, W. W. (2001). Observations on mortality during the 1918 influenza pandemic. *Clinical Infectious Diseases, 33*, 1375–1378.

Mamelund, S. E. (2003). Spanish influenza mortality of ethnic minorities in Norway 1918–1919. *European Journal of Population, 19*(1), 83–102.
Mamelund, S. E. (2006). A socially neutral disease? Individual social class, household wealth and mortality from Spanish influenza in two socially contrasting parishes in Kristiania 1918–19. *Social Science and Medicine, 62*(4), 923–940.
Mamelund, S. E. (2011). Geography may explain adult mortality from the 1918–20 influenza pandemic. *Epidemics, 3*, 46–60.
Mamelund, S. E. (2017). Social inequality—A forgotten factor in pandemic influenza preparedness. *Tidsskrift for Den norske legeforening.*
Mamelund, S. E. (2018). 1918 pandemic morbidity: The first wave hits the poor, the second wave hits the rich. *Influenza and Other Respiratory Viruses, 12*(3), 307–313.
Mamelund, S. E., Shelley-Egan, C., & Rogeberg, O. (2021). The association between socioeconomic status and pandemic influenza: Systematic review and meta-analysis. *PLoS ONE, 16*(9), e0244346.
Markel, H., Lipman, H. B., Navarro, J. A., Sloan, A., Michalsen, J. R., Stern, A. M., & Cetron, M. S. (2007). Nonpharmaceutical interventions implemented by US cities during the 1918–1919 influenza pandemic. *JAMA, 298*(6), 644–654.
Martínez-Carrión, J. M., & Moreno-Lázaro, J. (2007). Was there an urban height penalty in Spain, 1840–1913? *Economics and Human Biology, 5*, 144–164.
Martínez-Galarraga, J., Rosés, J. R., & Tirado, D. A. (2015). The long-term patterns of regional income inequality in Spain, 1860–2000. *Regional Studies, 49*(4), 502–517.
McCord, M., Lo, D., McCord, J., Davis, P., Haran, M., & Turley, P. (2022). The impact of COVID-19 on house prices in Northern Ireland: Price persistence, yet divergent? *Journal of Property Research*, forthcoming.
McNeill, W. H. (1977). *Plagues and people.* Basil Blackwell.
Mordechai, L., Eisenberg, M., Newfield, T. P., Izdebski, A., Kay, J. E., & Poinar, H. (2019). The Justinianic Plague: An inconsequential pandemic? *Proceedings of the National Academy of Sciences, 116*(51), 25546–25554.
Morozova, O. M., Troshina, T. I., Morozova, E. N., & Morozov, A. N. (2021). The Spanish flu pandemic in 1918 in Russia. Questions a hundred years later. *Journal of Microbiology, Epidemiology and Immunobiology, 98*(1), 113–124.
Murray, C. J., Lopez, A. D., Chin, B., Feehan, D., & Hill, K. H. (2007). Estimation of potential global pandemic influenza mortality on the basis of vital registry data from the 1918–20 pandemic: A quantitative analysis. *Lancet, 368*(9554), 2211–2218.
Murray, D. R., & Schaller, M. (2016). The behavioral immune system. *Advances in Experimental Social Psychology, 53*, 75–129.

Nettle, D. (2005). An evolutionary approach to the extraversion continuum. *Evolutionary Human Behavior, 26,* 363–373.
Nicolau, R. (2005). Población, salud y actividad. *Estadísticas históricas de España: siglo, XIX–XX*(I), 77–154.
North, D. C. (1981). *Structure and change in economic history.* W. W. Norton.
Noy, I., Okubo, T., & Strobl, E. (2020). The Japanese textile sector and the influenza pandemic of 1918–1920 (CESifo Working Papers, 8651).
Noymer, A., & Garenne, M. (2000). The 1918 influenza epidemic's effect on sex differentials in mortality in the United States. *Population and Development Review, 26*(3), 565–581.
Nuñez, C. E. (1989). *Alfabetización y crecimiento económico en la España contemporánea* (PhD thesis). University of Alcalá.
Økland, H., & Mamelund, S. E. (2019). Race and 1918 influenza pandemic in the United States: A review of the literature. *International Journal of Environmental Research and Public Health, 16*(14), 2487.
Oxford, J. S., Lambkin, R., Sefton, A., Daniels, R., Elliot, A., Brown, R., & Gill, D. (2005). A hypothesis: The conjunction of soldiers, gas, pigs, ducks, geese and horses in Northern France during the Great War provided the conditions for the emergence of the "Spanish" influenza pandemic of 1918–1919. *Vaccine, 23*(7), 940–945.
Pamuk, Ş. (2007). The Black Death and the origins of the 'Great Divergence' across Europe, 1300–1600. *European Review of Economic History, 11*(3): 289–317.
Parman, J. (2015). Childhood health and sibling outcomes: Nurture Reinforcing nature during the 1918 influenza pandemic. *Explorations in Economic History, 58*(91), 22–43.
Paskoff, T., & Sattenspiel, L. (2019). Sex-and age-based differences in mortality during the 1918 influenza pandemic on the island of Newfoundland. *American Journal of Human Biology, 31*(1), e23198.
Pearce, D. C., Pallaghy, P. K., McCaw, J. M., McVernon, J., & Mathews, J. D. (2011). Understanding mortality in the 1918–1919 influenza pandemic in England and Wales. *Influenza and Other Respiratory Viruses, 5*(2), 89–98.
Peel, M. C., Finlayson, B. L., & McMahon, T. A. (2007). Updated world map of the Köppen-Geiger climate classification. *Hydrology and Earth System Sciences, 11,* 1633–1644.
Pérez Moreda, V., Reher, D. S., & Gimeno, A. S. (2015). La conquista de la salud: Mortalidad y modernización en la España contemporánea. *Madrid, 75,* 87–110.
Porta, M. (Ed.). (2014). *A dictionary of epidemiology.* Oxford University Press.
Prados de la Escosura, L. (2017). *Spanish economic growth, 1850–2015.* Palgrave Macmillan.

Prados de la Escosura, L., & Rosés, J. R. (2009). The sources of long-run growth in Spain, 1850–2000. *Journal of Economic History, 69*(4), 1063–1091.

Prados de la Escosura, L., & Rosés, J. R. (2010). Long-run estimates of physical capital in Spain, 1850–2000. *Research in Economic History, 27,* 141–200.

Prados de la Escosura, L. P., & Sánchez-Alonso, B. (2020). Economic development in Spain, 1815–2017. In *Oxford research encyclopedia of economics and finance*. Oxford University Press.

Prem, H. (1991). Disease outbreaks in Central Mexico during the sixteenth century. In N. D. Cook & G. W. Lovello (Eds.), *Secret Judgments of God: Old World Disease in Colonial Spanish America* (pp. 20–48). Norman.

Ramani, A., & Bloom, N. (2021). The doughnut effect of Covid-19 on cities. *Vox CEPR Policy Portal.*

Ramiro, D., & Sanz, A. (1999). Cambios estructurales en la mortalidad infantil y juvenil en España, 1860–1930. *Boletín de la ADE, 17,* 40–87.

Reher, D. S. (2001). In search of the 'urban penalty': Exploring urban and rural mortality patterns in Spain during the demographic transition. *International Journal of Population Geography, 7,* 105–127.

Reher, D. S. (2011). Economic and social implications of the demographic transition. *Population and Development Review, 37*(1), 11–33.

Reinhart, C. M., & Rogoff, K. S. (2009). *This time is different: Eight centuries of financial folly.* Princeton University Press.

Rice, G. W., & Palmer, E. (1993). Pandemic influenza in Japan, 1918–19: Mortality patterns and official responses. *Journal of Japanese Studies, 19*(2), 389–420.

Richard, S. A., Sugaya, N., Simonsen, L., Miller, M. A., & Viboud, C. (2009). A comparative study of the 1918–1920 influenza pandemic in Japan, USA and UK: mortality impact and implications for pandemic planning. *Epidemiology and Infection, 137*(8), 1062e72.

Rodríguez Ocaña, E. (1994). La Salud Pública en España en el contexto europeo, 1890–1925. *Revista de Sanidad e Higiene Pública, 68,* 11–27.

Rose, C. S. (2021). Implications of the Spanish influenza pandemic (1918–1920) for the history of early 20th century Egypt. *Journal of World History, 32*(4), 655–684.

Rosen, W. (2007). *Justinian's Flea: The First Great Plague and the End of the Roman Empire.* Penguin.

Rosés, J. R., Martínez-Galarraga, J., & Tirado, D. A. (2010). The upswing of regional income inequality in Spain (1860–1930). *Explorations in Economic History, 47*(2), 244–257.

Rosés, J. R., & Sánchez-Alonso, B. (2004). Regional wage convergence in Spain 1850–1930. *Explorations in Economic History, 41*(4), 404–425.

Scheidel, W. (2017). *The great leveler: Violence and the history of inequality from the stone age to the twenty-first century.* Princeton University Press.

Schmelzing, P. (2020). *Eight centuries of global real rates, R-G, and the 'suprasecular' decline, 1311–2018* (Staff Working Papers, 845). Bank of England.
Schoenbaum, S. C. (1996). Impact of influenza in persons and populations. *Options for the Control of Influenza, III*, 17–25.
Shaw, I. W. (2020). *Pandemic: The Spanish Flu in Australia 1918–20*. Woodslane Press.
Shortridge, K. F. (1999). The 1918 'Spanish' flu: Pearls from swine? *Nature Medicine*, 5(4), 384–385.
Simonsen, L., Chowell, G., Andreasen, V., Gaffey, R., Barry, J., Olson, D., & Viboud, C. (2018). A review of the 1918 herald pandemic wave: Importance for contemporary pandemic response strategies. *Annals of Epidemiology*, 28(5), 281–288.
Singh, M. (2021). Bombay Fever/Spanish Flu: Public health and native press in Colonial Bombay, 1918–19. *South Asia Research*, 41(1), 35–52.
Spinney, L. (2017). *Pale rider: The Spanish flu of 1918 and how it changed the world*. Public Affairs.
Spychalski, P., Błażyńska-Spychalska, A., & Kobiela, J. (2020). Estimating case fatality rates of COVID-19. *Lancet Infectious Diseases*, 20(7), 774–775.
Stasavage, D. (2016). What we can learn from the early history of sovereign debt. *Explorations in Economic History*, 59(supp. C), 1–16.
Sudrià, C. (2021). A hidden fight behind neutrality. Spain's struggle on exchange rates and gold during the Great War. *European Review of Economic History*, 25(3), 549–570.
Sydenstricker, E. (1931). The incidence of influenza among persons of different economic status during the epidemic of 1918. *Public Health Reports (1896–1970)*, 154–170.
Takahashi, T., Ellingson, M. K., Wong, P., Israelow, B., Lucas, C., Klein, J., Silva, J., Mao, T., Oh, J. E., Tokuyama, M., & Lu, P. (2020). Sex differences in immune responses that underlie COVID-19 disease outcomes. *Nature*, 588(7837), 315–320.
Tamerius, J. D., Shaman, J., Alonso, W. J., Bloom-Feshbach, K., Uejio, C. K., Comrie, A., & Viboud, C. (2013). Environmental predictors of seasonal influenza epidemics across temperate and tropical climates. *PLOS Pathogens*, 9(3), e1003194.
Taubenberger, J. K., Kash, J. C., & Morens, D. M. (2019). The 1918 influenza pandemic: 100 years of questions answered and unanswered. *Science Translational Medicine*, 11(502).
Taubenberger, J. K., & Morens, D. (2006). 1918 influenza: The mother of all pandemics. *Emerging Infectious Diseases*, 12(1), 15–22.
Theilmann, J., & Cate, F. (2007). A plague of plagues: The problem of plague diagnosis in medieval England. *Journal of Interdisciplinary History*, 37(3), 371–393.

Tognotti, E. (2003). Scientific triumphalism and learning from facts: Bacteriology and the 'Spanish flu' challenge of 1918. *Social History of Medicine, 16*(1), 97–110.

Trilla, A., Trilla, G., & Daer, C. (2008). The 1918 "Spanish flu" in Spain. *Clinical Infectious Diseases, 47*(5), 668–673.

Tuckel, P., Sassler, S., Maisel, R., & Leykam, A. (2006). The diffusion of the influenza pandemic of 1918 in Hartford, Connecticut. *Social Science History, 30*(2), 167–196.

Turner-Musa, J., Ajayi, O., & Kemp, L. (2020, June). Examining social determinants of health, stigma, and COVID-19 disparities. *Healthcare, 8*(2), 168.

Vågene, Å. J., Herbig, A., Campana, M. G., Robles García, N. M., Warinner, C., Sabin, S., Spyrou, M. A., Andrades Valtueña, A., Huson, D., Tuross, N., Bos, K. I., & Krause, J. (2018). Salmonella enterica genomes from victims of a major sixteenth-century epidemic in Mexico. *Nature Ecology & Evolution, 2*(3), 520–528.

Vaughan, W. T. (1920). Influenza: An epidemiological study. *American Journal of Hygiene, iii*, 260

Velde, F. R. (2020). *What happened to the US economy during the 1918 influenza pandemic? A view through high-frequency data* (Federal Reserve Bank of Chicago Working Papers, 2020-11).

Viboud, C., Eisenstein, J., Reid, A. H., Janczewski, T. A., Morens, D. M., & Taubenberger, J. K. (2013). Age-and sex-specific mortality associated with the 1918–1919 influenza pandemic in Kentucky. *Journal of Infectious Diseases, 207*(5), 721–729.

Voigtländer, N., & Voth, H.-J. (2013). The three horsemen of riches: Plague, war, and urbanization in early modern Europe. *Review of Economic Studies, 80*(2), 774–811.

Weil, D. N. (2014). Health and economic growth. *Handbook of Economic Growth, 2*(3), 623–682.

Wilson, N., Oliver, J., Rice, G., Summers, J. A., Baker, M. G., Waller, M., & Shanks, G. D. (2014). Age-specific mortality during the 1918–19 influenza pandemic and possible relationship to the 1889–92 influenza pandemic. *Journal of Infectious Diseases, 210*(6), 993–995.

World Economic Outlook. (2021, October). *International Monetary Fund*. Imf Publications. https://www.imf.org/en/Publications/WEO/weo-database/2021/October

Wu, W. Q. (2020). The historical data of pandemic influenza in China from 1918 to 1920 in the Shun Pao. *Zhonghua yi shi za zhi, 50*(4), 225–237.

Young, A. (2005). The gift of the dying: The tragedy of aids and the welfare of future African generations. *Quarterly Journal of Economics, 120*(2), 423–466.

Index

A
Aassve, A., 45
Acemoglu, D., 61, 88
Acuña-Soto. R., 5, 14, 15
Aggregate output, 84, 85, 87–89, 91, 99
Alfani, G., 52, 61, 68, 69, 80, 88, 89
Almond, D., 94
Alonso, W.J., 45
Álvarez-Nogal, C., 53
Anderson, R.M., 43
Andreasen, V., 19, 28, 29, 45
Antonine Plague, 2–5
Arango, J., 61
Arthi, M.H., 99
AS-AD model, 84
Azizi, F., 28

B
Bailey, M., 98
Bambra, C., 43, 45
Barro, R., 25, 90, 91
Barry, J.M., 28, 29
Basco, S., 21, 22, 27, 39–41, 43–46, 58–62, 78, 80, 96, 99
Baud, D., 45
Beaney, T., 45
Bekaert, G., 95
Bengtsson, T., 39, 45, 94
Benmelech, E., 91
Berkes, E., 29
Bettencourt, L.M., 28, 45
Black Death, 2–4, 6, 8, 13, 14, 53, 54, 56, 68, 69, 80, 87–89, 98
Błażyńska-Spychalska, A., 45
Bloom, N., 98
Bloom-Feshbach, K., 45
Boianovsky, M., 99
Bolt, J., 10, 15
Bootsma, M.C.J., 25, 29
Bor, J., 45
Boserup, E., 98
Bowman, A., 6
Brainerd, E., 19
Bramanti, B., 6

© The Author(s), under exclusive license to Springer Nature Switzerland AG 2022
S. Basco et al., *Pandemics, Economics and Inequality*, Palgrave Studies in Economic History,
https://doi.org/10.1007/978-3-031-05668-0

Broadberry, S.N., 62, 89, 98
Brown, C., 45
Brundage, J.F., 46
Burdekin, R.C., 99
Byerly, C.R., 46

C
Cain, L., 46
Callegari, B., 99
Campbell, B., 98
Capital, 7, 13, 14, 21, 37, 40, 66, 69, 70, 76, 77, 79, 83, 84, 87, 88, 94, 97–99
  capital returns, 65, 66, 97
Caramelo, F., 45
Carillo, M.F., 91, 92
Carmona, J., 75, 80
Cate, F., 14
Chan, H.H.H., 46
Chandra, S., 28
Charu, V., 45
Chen, J.T., 45
Cheshire, P., 80
Chin, B., 46
Chowell, G., 28, 29, 45
Christakos, G., 4
Cilek, L., 28
Cirillo, P., 2, 3, 5, 54, 61
Clarke, J.C., 45
Clark, G., 61, 69
Clay, K., 45
Cleaveland, M.K., 5, 14, 15
Cobb-Douglas, 66, 67
Cocoliztli, 5, 15
Cohen-Kristiansen, R., 99
Collcutt, M., 15
Collier, R., 28
Colvin, C.L., 35
Correia, S., 91, 99
Court, V., 99
Covid-19, 2, 3, 8, 12–14, 37, 79, 90, 94–97

Credit Suisse, 97
Cummings, D.A., 39, 45

D
Daufenbach, L.Z., 45
Davis, S., 28
Dean, K.R., 6
Death toll, 2–6, 8, 9, 11, 13, 15, 54, 61
Deaton, A., 61
de la Macorra, L., 80
Demombynes, G., 45
De Pleijt, A.M., 98
De Santis, R.A., 90
Deschenes, O., 29
D'Lima, W., 80
Diffusion, 4, 21, 27, 29, 36, 42, 44
Domènech, J., 21, 22, 27, 39–41, 43–46, 58–62, 78, 96

E
Echeverri-Dávila, B., 28, 29, 45
Economic crises, 11, 55, 98
Economic growth, 10, 25, 89, 98
Eisenberg, M., 14
Elgar, F.J., 45
Eloranta, J., 99
Engstrom, E., 95
Eriksson, B., 39
Erkoreka, A., 45
Ermolov, A., 95
Erreygers, G., 99
Evans, R., 46
Excess flu mortality, 54
Excess mortality, 3, 19, 20, 34–42, 44, 46, 55, 58–62, 74, 79, 90, 92, 93

F
Farris, W.W., 6

INDEX   121

Favre, G., 45
Feder, C., 99
Feigenbaum, J., 45
Female penalty, 37
Ferguson, N.M., 25, 29
Ferreira, N., 45
Flores, J., 28, 29, 45
Ford, J., 43, 45
Fortson, J.G., 7
Friedman, M., 12
Frydman, C., 91

G
Gaetani, R., 29
Gaffey, R., 19, 28, 29, 45
Gallardo-Albarrán, D., 28, 91
Gallent, N., 80
Galletta, S., 57
Galor, O., 61
Gandolfi, F., 45
García Delgado, J.L., 62
Garenne, M., 36
Gil Ibáñez, S., 45
Gimeno, A.S., 29, 61
Giommoni, T., 57
Glass, G.E., 39, 45
Goerlich Gisbert, F.J., 40
Golestaneh, A.K., 45
Grantham, G.W., 98
Grantz, K.H., 39, 45
Great Leveler, 97
Great Recession, 8, 10–12, 66
Great War, 12, 26, 54, 55, 57, 62
Gross, P., 45
Guan, D., 96
Guimbeau, A., 94

H
Haines, M.R., 42, 46
Hallegatte, S., 96
Harper, K., 89

Harrison, M., 62, 99
Hatcher, J., 98
Hatchett, R.J., 29
Helgertz, J., 94
Herrera-Diestra, J.L., 46
Herring, D.A., 45
Hilber, C., 80
Hirano, E.W, 45
HIV/AIDS, 3, 6, 7
Hodgson, A., 37
Hong, S.C., 46, 94
House prices, 72, 74–77, 97
Housing, 13, 37, 66, 69–77, 79, 80, 83, 97, 100
 housing demand, 14, 70–72, 75–77, 79
 housing market, 70–73, 75, 80
 housing supply, 70–73, 76

I
IMF, 96, 97
Income distribution, 14
Inequality, 7, 13, 51–53, 57, 62, 65, 68, 69, 96, 97, 100
Influenza, 3, 5, 8, 13, 14, 18–24, 27, 29, 34, 35, 37, 39, 42–44, 57, 91, 94
Institutions, 21, 26, 28, 69, 73, 88, 89, 98
Italy, 4, 6, 8–11, 15, 53, 57, 62, 69, 89, 92

J
Jain, V., 45
Japan, 3, 6, 9, 10, 18, 19, 27, 28, 91
Jappelli, T., 91, 92
Jay, J., 45
Jedwab, R., 4, 53, 89, 99
Johnson, N., 5, 8, 9, 27, 61, 62
Jones, C.I., 7
Jordà, Ò., 53, 66, 69

K
Karlsson, M., 28, 57, 91
Kash, J.C., 45
Kassens-Noor, E., 28
Keeling, A.W., 46
Keynes, J.M., 62
Klein, S.L., 37, 98
Klenow, P.J., 7
Knoll, K., 66
Kobiela, J., 45
Kolata, G., 28
Korol, E., 45
Koudijs, P., 98
Koyama, M., 4, 53, 89, 99
Krieger, N., 45
Kuljanin, G., 28
Kuvshinov, D., 66
Kwok, K.O., 46

L
Labour, 7, 52, 53, 69, 72, 75, 76, 79, 83, 87, 88, 98
 labour demand, 52, 56, 57, 61, 84
 labour market, 13, 40, 55–58, 60, 65, 76, 88
 labour supply, 55–58, 61
Lacomba, J.A., 80
Lambkin, R., 28
Lampe, M., 75, 80
Land, 6, 13, 52, 66–73, 76, 79, 80, 84, 87, 89
 land returns, 66–69, 80
Lee, R., 61
Le Moglie, M., 45
Lewis, J., 45
Li, K.K., 46
Lin, J., 29
Lipman, H.B., 25, 26, 29, 37
Lipsitch, M., 29
Lo, D., 80
Long-run, 4, 6, 7, 14, 53, 58, 60, 71, 74, 84, 85, 87–89, 91–94, 98

Lopez, L.A., 80
Luck, S., 91, 99
Luk, L., 45
Lyons, G., 45

M
Madeddu, M., 80
Majeed, A., 45
Malthusian, 51–54, 66, 67, 69, 70, 80, 87, 89
Mamelund, S.E., 39, 45
Markel, H., 25, 26, 29, 37
Martínez-Carrión, J.M., 42
Martínez-Galarraga, J., 62
Matthews, F., 43, 45
May, R.M., 43
McCaw, J.M., 29
McCord, J., 80
McCord, M., 80
McLaughlin, E., 35
Mecher, C.E., 29
Menon, N., 94
Mestieri, M., 99
Mexico, 3, 5, 9, 14, 18, 27, 96
Meyers, L.A., 46
Miller, M.A., 28, 29, 45
Mordechai, L., 14
Moreno-Lázaro, J., 42
Morens, D., 14, 28
Morozova, O.M., 28
Mortgage, 73, 74, 76
 mortgage credit, 78
Mueller, J., 5, 8, 9, 27, 61, 62
Muller, C., 45
Muñoz, J., 62
Murphy, T., 88, 89
Murray, D.R., 46
Musacchio, A., 94
Musso, D., 45

N

Navarro, J.A., 25, 26, 29, 37
Nettle, D., 46
Newfield, T.P., 14
Newspapers, 13, 20–24, 26, 29, 44, 60
Nicolau, R., 45
Nielsen-Saines, K., 45
Nilsson, T., 28, 57, 91
Nonpharmacological interventions, 27
North, D.C., 98
Noy, I., 91
Noymer, A., 36
Nsoesie, E.O., 45
Nuñez, C.E., 40

O

Occupations, 13, 36, 40–42, 44–46, 57–60, 75
Økland, H., 45
Okubo, T., 91
Olea, R., 4
Overton, M., 98
Oxford, J.S., 28

P

Pallaghy, P.K., 29
Palmer, E., 28
Parman, J., 94, 99
Pearce, D.C., 29
Pérez Moreda, V., 29, 61
Persistence, 69, 74, 92
Pichler, S., 28, 57, 91
Pinheiro, R., 99
Plague, 2, 4–6, 14, 53, 54, 61, 89
  Plague of Justinian, 3, 4, 6
Pomar, L., 45
Porta, M., 35
Pradhan, A., 80
Prados de la Escosura, L., 11, 61, 70, 79, 86, 92

Pre-industrial, 13, 52, 61, 66, 67, 69, 79, 88, 89, 97, 98
Prem, H., 5
Productivity, 52, 53, 56, 66, 67, 79, 84, 86–88
Public, 21, 27, 41, 44, 55, 73, 80
  public health, 4, 25
  public interventions, 25

Q

Qi, X., 45

R

Raees, G.H., 28
Ramiro Fariñas, D., 28
Rane, M.S., 39, 45
Ravallion, M., 45
Real wages, 13, 14, 51–62, 65, 68, 72, 74, 75, 89, 92, 94
Reher, D.S., 46, 61
Rice, G.W., 28
Richard, S.A., 28
Riordan, R., 43, 45
Robinson, D.P., 37
Robinson, J., 61
Rogeberg, O., 39
Roldán, S., 62
Rome, 4, 5
Rose, C.S., 28
Rosen, W., 14
Rosés, J.R., 11, 40, 46, 62, 70, 79, 92
Ruiz, A., 80
Ruiz, G., 80
Rural, 27, 42–45, 54, 76–78, 92–94, 99
  rural credit, 77
  rural penalty, 42

S

Salje, H., 39, 45

Salman, D., 45
Sánchez-Alonso, B., 46, 61
Santiago Caballero, C., 80
Sanz, A., 46
Schachterle, S.E., 39, 45
Schaller, M., 46
Scheidel, W., 14, 15, 53
Schmelzing, P., 69
Schoenbaum, S.C., 45
Schöni, O., 80
Schularick, M., 53, 66, 69
Schwartz, A., 12
Sefton, A., 28
Serre, M., 4
Severen, C., 29
Severnini, E., 45
Shaman, J., 45
Shanks, G.D., 46
Shaw, I.W., 28
Shelley-Egan, C., 39
Shortridge, K.F., 28
Short-run, 14, 58, 60, 62, 71, 76, 84–92, 95
Siegler, M., 19
Simonsen, L., 19, 28, 29, 45
Singh, M., 28
Singh, S.R., 53, 69
Sloan, A., 25, 26, 29, 37
Smallpox, 5, 6
 smallpox epidemic, 3, 5, 6
Social class, 97
Social distancing, 42–45, 92
Spain, 4, 5, 9, 11, 13, 18–21, 23, 26–29, 35, 37, 38, 40–45, 53–55, 58–62, 72–80, 86, 89, 92, 93, 95, 99
Spanish flu, 2, 3, 5–14, 18, 20, 28, 34, 36, 45, 54, 55, 57–62, 69, 72, 74, 77, 79, 88, 90–92, 94–97
Spinney, L., 28
Spychalski, P., 45
Stahle, D.W., 5, 14, 15

Stasavage, D., 69
Stefaniak, A., 45
Stenseth, N.C., 6
Strobl, E., 91
Structural change, 71, 87, 99
Sudrià, C., 62
Sugaya, N., 28
Sweden, 9, 11, 18, 19, 28, 39, 57, 91, 94
Sydenstricker, E., 45

T
Taleb, N.N., 2, 3, 5, 54, 61
Tamerius, J., 45
Taubenberger, J.K., 14, 28, 45
Taylor, A.M., 53, 66, 69
Technological change, 7, 88
Theilmann, J., 14
Therrell, M.D., 5, 14, 15
Thompson, W.W., 45
Tirado, D.A., 40, 62, 79
Tognotti, E., 29
Trilla, A., 19, 21, 26, 27, 29
Troshina, T.I., 28
Tuckel, P., 45
Turan, B., 7
Turner-Musa, J., 45

U
Uncertainty, 80, 84, 87, 94, 95, 98
Unequal, 13, 36, 45, 54
United Kingdom, 11
United States, 9, 12, 18, 19, 24–27, 57, 58, 77, 79, 91, 94, 95, 97, 99, 100
Urban, 26, 42–46, 54, 60, 73, 76–78, 92–94, 99
 urban credit, 77–79
 urban penalty, 42
Ursúa, J., 25, 90, 91

V
Vagene, A.J., 14
van der Veken, W., 90
van Leeuwen, B., 98
van Zanden, J.L., 10, 15, 98
Vaughan, W.T., 45
Velde, F.R., 91, 92
Verner, E., 91, 99
Viboud, C., 28
Voigtländer, N., 89
Voth, H-J., 89, 98

W
Walløe, L., 6
Wang, D., 96
Wang, L., 4
Way, J., 28
Weil, D.N., 98

Weng, J., 25, 90, 91
Wilson, N., 45
Wohl, M.J., 45
World War I, 11, 12, 15, 19, 35, 73, 90, 92, 95, 96
Wrigley-Field, E., 45
Wu, W.Q., 28

Y
Yi, Y.Y., 46
Young, A., 7
Yu, H., 4
Yun, Y., 94

Z
Zwart, P., 91